Intellectual Property Law in Kenya

Intellectual Property Law in Kenya

Isaac Rutenberg
Marisella Ouma
Peter Munyi

This book was originally published as a monograph in the International Encyclopaedia of Laws/Intellectual Property Law.

Founding Editor: Roger Blanpain
General Editor: Frank Hendrickx
Volume Editor: Hendrik Vanhees

Wolters Kluwer

Published by:
Kluwer Law International B.V.
PO Box 316
2400 AH Alphen aan den Rijn
The Netherlands
E-mail: international-sales@wolterskluwer.com
Website: lrus.wolterskluwer.com

Sold and distributed in North, Central and South America by:
Wolters Kluwer Legal & Regulatory U.S.
7201 McKinney Circle
Frederick, MD 21704
United States of America
Email: customer.service@wolterskluwer.com

Sold and distributed in all other countries by:
Air Business Subscriptions
Rockwood House
Haywards Heath
West Sussex
RH16 3DH
United Kingdom
Email: international-customerservice@wolterskluwer.com

Printed on acid-free paper

ISBN 978-94-035-1740-7

e-Book: ISBN 978-94-035-1783-4
web-PDF: ISBN 978-94-035-1831-2

Printed in the United Kingdom.

The Authors

Isaac Rutenberg is an academic and lawyer based in Nairobi, Kenya. He is currently the Director of the Centre for Intellectual Property and Information Technology Law (CIPIT) at the Strathmore Law School, Strathmore University, where he is also a senior lecturer. Isaac holds a JD (degree in law), a PhD in Chemistry, a Bachelor of Science in Chemistry, and a Bachelor of Science in Mathematics/Computer Science. He is admitted to practice law in the state of California, patent law in the United States Patent and Trademark Office (USPTO), and patent/trademark law in the Kenya Industrial Property Institute (KIPI). He is a member of the Chartered Institute of Arbitrators (Kenya Branch) and the American Chemical Society. He also served as a member of the Board of Directors at the Kenya Copyright Board (KECOBO).

Marisella Ouma is a lawyer and an advocate of the High Court of Kenya, with expertise in Intellectual Property (IP) Law based in Nairobi, Kenya. She is currently the Head of Legal at the Central Bank of Kenya and has been a part-time/visiting lecturer at the University of Nairobi, Strathmore University and the Africa University. She is also an online tutor at the World Intellectual Property Organization (WIPO) Academy. She holds a PhD in Law from Queen Mary, University of London. She is a Member of the Law Society of Kenya and the Institute of Certified Secretaries in Kenya. She previously worked as the Deputy Solicitor General, Legal Advisory and Research, Office of the Attorney General and Department of Justice and was the founding Executive Director of the KECOBO. She has also served on the Board of the KIPI as well as the Board of the Anti-Counterfeit Agency (ACA).

The Authors

Peter Munyi is a lawyer in academia and practice. He is a lecturer at the School of Law, University of Nairobi, and a visiting lecturer at Strathmore Law School, Strathmore University, both in Nairobi. His legal practice focuses on all aspects of IP and related issues. Peter holds a PhD from Wageningen University & Research, the Netherlands; a Master's degree in European Intellectual Property Law from Stockholm University, Sweden and a Bachelor's degree in Law from Moi University, Kenya. He is a member of the Licensing Executives Society.

Table of Contents

Table of Contents

List of Abbreviations

ACA	Anti-counterfeit Agency
ARIPO	African Regional Intellectual Property Organization
CBD	Convention on Biological Diversity
CIA	Central Intelligence Agency
CMOs	Collective Management Organizations
CSIP	Centre for Scientific and Industrial Research
DPP	Director of Public Prosecutions
EU	European Union
GIs	Geographical Indications
GR	Genetic Resources
IP	Intellectual Property
IPA	Industrial Property Act
IPIC Treaty	Integrated Property in Respect of Integrated Circuits Treaty
IPR	Intellectual Property Rights
IPT	Industrial Property Tribunal
ISP	Internet Service Providers or Intermediary Service Providers
ITPGRFA	International Treaty on Plant Genetic Resources for Food and Agriculture
KAMP	Kenya Association of Music Producers
KECOBO	Kenya Copyright Board
KEPHIS	Kenya Plant Health Inspectorate Service
KIPI	Kenya Industrial Property Institute
KIPO	Kenya Industrial Patent Office
KOPIKEN	Reprographic Rights Organisation of Kenya
MCSK	Music Copyright Society of Kenya
MPAKE	Music Publishers Association of Kenya
PCT	Patent Cooperation Treaty
PRiSK	Performers Rights Society of Kenya
PVR	Plant Varieties Protection
TCE	Traditional Cultural Expressions Policy
TK	Traditional Knowledge

List of Abbreviations

TRIPS	Trade-Related Aspects of Intellectual Property Rights
UK	United Kingdom
UMC	Utility Model Certificate
UNESCO	United Nations Educational, Scientific and Cultural Organization
UPOV	International Convention for the Protection of New Varieties of Plants
US	United States
USPTO	United States Patent and Trademark Office
WCT	WIPO Copyright Treaty
WIPO	World Intellectual Property Organization
WPPT	WIPO Performances and Phonograms Treaty
WTO	World Trade Organisation

List of Figures and Table

List of Figures and Table

Preface

'Intellectual Property Law Kenya' is a monograph that offers a systematic look at Intellectual Property Rights (IPR) in the Kenyan context. Throughout much of the twentieth century, IPR operated in the exclusive realm of developed nations and big businesses. This began to change towards the end of the century, first in the higher developing BRICS countries, and more recently in middle developing countries. Today, IPR form the cornerstone of the modern economy, and all but a few countries recognise that there can be no sustained development without effective, country-wide use of intellectual property (IP) systems.

This monograph is an introduction and practical manual for IPR and the systems that deliver and protect such rights. Due to the international nature of IP, each topic includes discussions on international aspects of the rights and concepts under review. Uniquely among international IP texts, this monograph approaches the subject matter from a Kenyan perspective.

Ultimately this monograph offers judges, advocates, scholars, and law students an in-depth analysis and broad introduction to IPR from the Kenyan perspective, with a robust and yet concise account of the types, interaction, and operation of various IPR.

Preface

General Introduction

§1. General Background

I. Geography

1. The Republic of Kenya is a country in East Africa. Straddling the equator, Kenya has over 400 km of coastline along the Indian Ocean to the east, and over 100 km of coastline along Lake Victoria to the southwest.[1] Neighbouring countries are Uganda to the west, South Sudan to the north-west, Ethiopia to the north and north-east, Somalia to the east, and Tanzania to the south. Kenya has a land mass measuring 580,367 km^2 (224,080 mi) and its economy, like those of most African and developing countries, is heavily dependent on agriculture.[2] The country is named after Mount Kenya, a significant landmark and the second highest mountain peak in Africa.

2. Kenya is currently home to seven World Heritage Sites, including the Kenya Lake System in the Great Rift Valley, and the Mount Kenya National Park.[3] The Maasai Mara is an animal refuge in the Great Rift Valley that includes some of the largest and most well-known concentrations of large mammals in Africa. Major cities in Kenya, in decreasing order of population, are Nairobi, Mombasa, Kisumu, and Nakuru.

3. Prior to 2010, the country was divided into eight provinces. Under the Constitution of Kenya 2010, the provinces were dissolved and the country is now divided into forty-seven counties. Each county may be further subdivided into one or more districts. The four largest counties by area are located in the northern and eastern regions: Turkana, Marsabit, Wajir, and Garissa. The four smallest counties by area are Mombasa, Vihiga, Nairobi, and Nyamira. A map of Kenya is shown in Figure 1. The national flag and coat of arms, both provided in the Constitution of Kenya 2010, are shown in Figure 2.

---

1. Google Earth.
2. Mwakikagile G, (2007) *Kenya: Identity of a Nation*, Pretoria, SA: New African Press.
3. United Nations Educational, Scientific and Cultural Organization (UNESCO).

Figure 1 Map of Kenya[4]

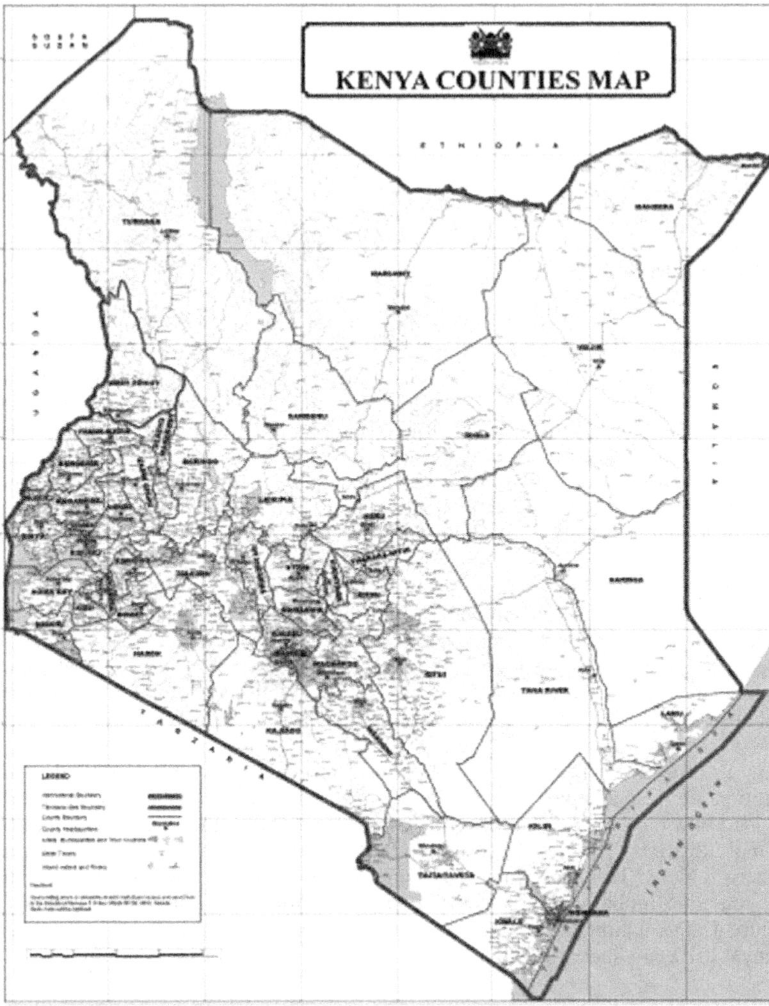

4. Source: Survey of Kenya, Ministry of Lands, Government of Kenya.

Figure 2 Kenya's National Flag and Coat of Arms[5]

II. Cultural Composition

4. The people of Kenya are predominantly descended from three ethnic groups: the Bantu, the Cushite, and the Nilotes. Many ethnic communities in Kenya are recognised as having descended from these groups, although the classification of such ethnic communities in Kenya is complex. The Kenya National Bureau of Statistics provides population statistics for dozens of ethnicities, the largest of which are the Kikuyu, Luhya, Kalenjin, Luo, and Kamba.[6]

5. There is freedom of religion in Kenya. Although there is no state religion,[7] the two largest religions are Christian (83% of the population) and Muslim (11% of the population).[8]

6. The aspect of culture that is most specifically recognised and preserved in the Constitution of Kenya 2010 is that of language. The 'national language' is Kiswahili, even though the official languages are Kiswahili and English.[9] Furthermore, in recognition that the various ethnic communities have unique languages, the Constitution of Kenya 2010 specifically requires the State to protect the diversity of language and to promote the development and use of indigenous language.[10]

---

5. Source: Constitution of Kenya 2010.
6. Many ethnic communities in Kenya, including the Luhya and Kalenjin, are agglomerations of numerous ethnic communities, typically with shared language, history, or other characteristics. For population statistics, *see* the Kenya National Bureau of Statistics website (www.knbs.or.ke) and publications listed on that site.
7. Constitution of Kenya 2010, Art. 8.
8. Central Intelligence Agency (CIA), The World Factbook, Kenya chapter, 2009 estimates.
9. Constitution of Kenya 2010, Art. 7.
10. *Ibid.*

III. Political System

7. The Constitution of Kenya 2010 provides for a partially national and partially devolved system of government. Each county has a separate government, including executive and legislative branches. The governments at the national and county levels are distinct yet interdependent and are expected to cooperatively govern through consultation.[11]

8. The national government consists of independent executive, legislative, and judicial branches. The national legislature is a parliamentary system, and the Parliament of Kenya consists of the National Assembly and the Senate. The National Assembly 'deliberates on and resolves issues of concern to the people', and enacts legislation (particularly with respect to expenditure by national government and related organs).[12] The Senate represents and protects the interests of the counties, participates in law-making by approving bills that affect the counties, and allocates national revenues among the various counties.[13] By popular vote, each county elects one member of the Senate, and each constituency elects one member of the National Assembly. The remaining members of Parliament include women representatives and representatives of the youth and disabled, as determined by the Constitution of Kenya 2010.[14]

9. The national executive comprises a President, Deputy President, and Cabinet. The President is the Head of State, Head of Government, and Commander-in-Chief of the Kenya Defence Forces. The current President is H.E. Uhuru Kenyatta, and the Deputy President is H.E. William Ruto.

10. The history of political parties in Kenya is long and complicated, with origins in the period of colonial rule. The party of the current President and Deputy President is the Jubilee Party of Kenya, which was created in 2016 with the merger of a number of existing parties.

11. General elections, in which the President and all members of Parliament are elected by popular vote, are held every five years. The next election is scheduled for 2022.

IV. Population Statistics

12. The population of Kenya has been growing steadily at 2–4% for over fifty years, as shown from census data in Table 1. The last official figure, from 2009, provides an overall population density of 66.4 persons per square kilometre, although

11. Constitution of Kenya 2010, Art. 6.
12. Constitution of Kenya 2010, Art. 95.
13. Constitution of Kenya 2010, Art. 96.
14. Constitution of Kenya 2010, Arts 97–98.

the distribution of the population is greatly heterogeneous. For example, the population density of Nairobi County is 4,515 persons per square kilometre, while for Marsabit County it is only four persons per square kilometre. A new census is planned for mid-2019, and it is expected that the population of Kenya will exceed 50 million.

Table 1 Kenya Population Data[15]

	1948	*1962*	*1969*	*1979*	*1989*	*1999*	*2009*
Population (millions)	5.4	8.6	10.9	15.3	21.4	28.7	38.6
Size (1948=100)	100	159	202	283	396	532	715
Annual growth rate (% p.a.)	2.5	3.0	3.3	3.8	3.3	2.9	3.0

§2. Historical Background

13. Although various IP laws can be traced back through many centuries, the global move towards a more uniform system of IPR, including 'national treatment' (treatment by a government/law of foreign nationals the same as their own citizens), did not gain traction until the later part of the nineteenth century. At that time, national treatment became standard by the adoption of major international treaties such as the Paris Convention for Industrial Property and the Berne Convention for literary and artistic works.

14. An interesting trend that can be observed throughout the nineteenth and twentieth centuries is the ability of international pressure to alter the laws providing IPR within a country. Early examples of this can be seen in the adoption of patent laws, where highly innovative countries push their trading partners and/or bordering countries to provide legal protection for such innovation. Switzerland, for example, had limited patent protection until pressure from neighbouring Germany prevailed in forcing adoption of patent protection.[16] This trend of international pressure was strengthened with the adoption of the 1994 Trade-Related Aspects of Intellectual Property Rights (TRIPS) Agreement that, despite and over the objections of many developing countries, required uniformity in many aspects of IPR protection.

15. Until the late twentieth century, Kenyan IP laws were almost entirely based on the law of the United Kingdom (UK). As will be described throughout this text, by the early part of the twenty-first century, Kenya had developed a comprehensive suite of localised IP laws.

15. Kenya 2009 Population and Housing Census. Analytical Report on Population Dynamics. Vol. III. Kenya Population Situation Analysis, published by the Government of Kenya, 2013.
16. UK IPRs Commission Report, Integrating IPRs and Development Policy, 2002.

§3. Conclusion

16. Our journey into the study of IP law must begin with the understanding that these laws are continually evolving and attempting to deal with the complex subject matter to which they pertain. Definitions are often contested, contradictory, or entirely absent, leading to much debate among practitioners and academics over the meaning and implications of the law. In the East African context, IP law has, historically, has not been given much attention until very recently. This text provides a very high-level discussion of a wide variety of IPR, and interested readers are highly encouraged to seek out more in-depth discussions for areas of particular interest.

Intellectual Property Law

Chapter 1. Copyright and Neighbouring Rights

§1. Introduction and Theory

17. Copyright is a branch of IP that mainly protects the creative works such as books, songs, films, software and visual arts. Traditionally, copyright-protected literary and artistic works but was later expanded to include other works due to ever-changing technologies over the years. The intangible property protected by copyright is distinctive and unlike other IP it confers automatically for the benefit of the author.[17] Copyright grants the author the exclusive rights to exploit the works for a specific period of time subject to exceptions and limitations.

18. Related rights (neighbouring rights) are rights granted to performers, producers of sound recordings and broadcasting organisations. They rely on the underlying copyright works and the protection is mainly for the technical and organisational skill as well as investments made. This chapter provides an overview of copyright and related rights from the international as well as the national perspective.

19. The protection of copyright can be traced back to the 1710 Statute of Anne in England, which sought to protect the interests of the stationers. Over the years the protection was extended to include other works. Two systems of copyright developed, namely the authors' right system and the copyright system as will be discussed below. Technological advances and more recently the rapid advances in digital technology influenced development of copyright law. It should be noted that these two systems form the basis of most current national laws. The main difference between the two systems is that the '*droit d'auteur*' (author's right) system within the civil law jurisdictions placed emphasis on the author the individuality of the author. The common law system's, on the other hand, emphasis is on the economic

17. Bently L. Sherman B (2014) *Intellectual Property Law* 4th Edition, UK, Oxford University Press pp. 31.

aspect of the work. The *'droit d'auteur'* system is based on principles of natural justice while the common law system lays emphasis on the economic argument of property; it is more concerned with the commercial right.[18]

20. In Kenya, copyright law evolved from the 1842 UK Copyright Act through the 1911 and subsequently the 1956 UK Copyright Acts of the UK. Kenya enacted its first Copyright Act in 1966, which was based on the 1956 UK Copyright Act. It was amended several times to align it to the international instruments namely the Berne Convention. The 2001 Act, repealed the 1966 Act and ensured that Kenya was TRIPS compliant.[19]

21. The intangible nature of copyright makes it possible for several people to have the same copy at the same time. It is possible to access copyright-protected material online through social media, websites and other access *fora* over digital media. With the ever-changing digital technologies, the reproduction and distribution as well as access of works has been made easier as long as one has the necessary technology. This raises issues of control and authorisation for use of works as one can easily access without getting the relevant permission. Due to its nature and the potential for copyright to be easily accessed as well as have access restricted, it is necessary to constantly reassess its legitimacy.[20] Is copyright still necessary? How has it adopted to technological developments and how do the rights holder benefit without inhibiting access or taking into account public interest? There are five main arguments that are used to justify copyright but this chapter shall only deal with the main ones namely the economic rights and natural rights theory.[21]

I. Economic Theory

22. Under the economic theory, copyright protection is there to ensure that creativity is promoted by rewarding the creative authors and at the same time ensure access by users. It creates a balance between the rights of the authors/rights holders and the interests of the users of copyright works. Copyright like other IP protection is deemed to stimulate creativity through the production and distribution of knowledge and culture.[22] It assumes that without protection, there would be minimal creativity. It prevents free riding thus encouraging creativity by granting the authors

18. For Further reading *see* Sterling. J.A.L (2003). *World Copyright Law*, London: Sweet and Maxwell p. 55. Gillian Davies. (2002). *Copyright and the Public Interest*. London: Sweet and Maxwell, pp. 9–17.
19. *Ibid.*, p. 32.
20. *Ibid.*, p. 35.
21. For more comprehensive readings on the rationale and justification of Intellectual Property in general and on copyright, *see* Lehmann. M (1985). Theory of Property rights and the Protection of Intellectual and Industrial Property, *IIC* 16, May C. (2000). *Global Political Economy of Intellectual Property Rights*. Routledge: London, Hettinger E. (1997). 'Justifying Intellectual Property Law'. In Adam More. (ed). *Intellectual Property: Moral and Legal Dilemmas*. Lanham, Oxford.
22. Ouma M. (2010) Enforcement of Copyright and Related Rights in the Music industry on sub Saharan Africa PhD Thesis Queen Mary University of London.

property rights.[23] Copyright creates a system where the copyright owner is granted exclusive rights to use or exploit his work to compensate and reward him for his creativity and to provide an incentive for further creativity.[24] For instance, the author of software will have an incentive to create more software if the first one is protected from unauthorised use and he can exploit the same in the market. In countries like the United States (US), South Korea and India, the copyright industries are well developed due to the existing copyright protection system. On the contrary, countries like Kenya are yet to fully embrace copyright protection and have weak copyright industries:

> Copyright law exists to provide a marketable right for the creators and distributors of copyrighted works, which in turn creates a marketable right for the creators and distributors of copyrighted works, which in turn creates and incentive for production and dissemination of new works.[25]

23. This argument forms the basis of the copyright system.[26]

24. The question as to whether copyright stimulates production and distribution of knowledge and culture is debatable as in the pre copyright era; this was still possible without the encumbrances conferred by the legal system. The growth of the cultural industries and the dissemination of knowledge in countries with little or no copyright protection indicate otherwise. More recently, there have been arguments put forward that copyright impedes the dissemination of knowledge, especially in the developing countries due to the high cost of obtaining the knowledge from the rights holders. The lack of protection does not necessarily hinder the creative mind especially in the music industry, instead the creators continue to produce music but supplement their income from other sources. However, for other rights holders such as the record companies and publishers, copyright protection provides an incentive as they are more concerned with the economic returns and would be unwilling to invest in an industry that is full of risks and their rights are not legally secured. There are however societies where creative works thrived even when there was no copyright protection present. In pre-colonial Africa, copyright industries continued to exist although not as robust as in places with strong copyright protection.[27]

---

23. For further reading on creativity, incentive and rewards, *see* Ruth Towse, (2001). *Creativity, Incentive and Reward.* Edward Elgar UK, pp. 1–23.
24. Fisher William. (2001). Theories of International Property. In Stephen Munzer. (ed). *New Essays in Legal and Political Theory of Property.* William M. Landes and Richard A. Posner, (1989) 'An Economic Analysis of Copyright Law', 18 *J. Legal. Stud.* 325 available at http://www.law.harvard.edu /faculty/tfisher/iptheory.html.
25. Julie Cohen et al. (2002) *Copyright in a Global Economy.* New York: Aspen Law p. 7.
26. The economic justification been viewed with scepticism by some judicial authorities. (*See* the *obiter dictum, Biotech Laboratories (Pty) Ltd. v. Beecham Group PLC another* 2002 (4) SA 249 (SCA), at p. 259).
27. Ouma M. 2008 Enforcement of Copyright in the Music Industry: A Critical Analysis of the Legal and institutional Framework on Enforcement in Sub Saharan Africa: Doctoral Thesis, Queen Mary University of London.

II. Natural Rights Theory

25. Under the natural rights theory, copyright is to secure the author's economic interests and protect the works against any uses that may be prejudicial to the interests of the author. It is based on the premise that the creative works are an extension of the author's persona and should be protected as such. For example, a song that has been composed by an author is deemed to be the product of their mind, result of their intellectual effort and creativity. It explains the individual creativity. It is also based on the Locke's idea that a person has a natural right over the products of their intellectual labour.[28] This is the civil law *droit d'auteur* model, which seeks to ensure the protection of the economic rights as well as to guard against uses of the protected works in a manner that would be prejudicial to the interests of the authors.

26. Natural rights arguments centre on the person of the author who is thought to deserve a just reward for his/her intellectual labour or have a natural right in their creations. Thus, whoever invests in time and effort in the production of goods and services is entitled to the exclusive rights in them.[29] Prof Jane Ginsburg summed it as hereunder:

> Post revolutionary French laws and theorists portray the existence of an intimate and almost sacred bond between authors and their works as the source of a strong literary and artistic property right. Thus, France's leading modern exponent of copyright theory, the late Henri Desbois, grandly proclaimed: 'the author is protected as an author, in his status as a creator, because a bond unites him to the object of his creation.' In the French tradition, Parliament has repudiated the utilitarian concept of protecting works of authorship in order to stimulate literary and artistic activity.[30]

27. Copyright laws in Africa are modelled along these two approaches. It is interesting to note that countries with the civil law tradition have more vibrant copyright industries than the common law countries save for South Africa and more recently Kenya and Nigeria.

28. Both the economic and natural rights approach are embodied in the Universal Declaration of Human Rights of 1948. Article 17 protects the rights to ownership of property as well as guarantees the freedom against arbitrary deprivation of property. Article 27(1) grants the rights for everyone to freely participate in the cultural life of the community and enjoy the arts as well as share the scientific advances

28. For further reading *see* Breakey H. (2012) *Intellectual Liberty: Natural Rights and Intellectual Liberty* Yen A. 'Restoring the Natural Law: Copyright as Labour and Possession' (1990) *Ohio St LJ 517.*
29. Ouma M. 2008 Enforcement of Copyright in the Music Industry: A Critical Analysis of the Legal and institutional Framework on Enforcement in Sub Saharan Africa: Doctoral Thesis, Queen Mary University of London.
30. Ginsburg. J. (1990) A Tale of Two Copyrights: Literary Property in Revolutionary France and America, 64 *Tul. L. Rev.* 991, 992.

and benefits. It covers both the individual and public participation in the production, distribution and consumptive processes in society. Several legal systems in Africa have adopted a similar approach to copyright protection. They provide for both economic and moral rights of the author.[31]

29. Prof Goldstein in addressing the issue of the philosophical foundations of law noted the following:

> On one side are lawyers who assert that copyright is rooted in natural justice, entitling the authors to every last penny that other people will pay to obtain copies for their works. These are the copyright optimists: they view copyright's cup of entitlement as always half full, only waiting to be filled still further. On the other side of debate are copyright pessimists, who see copyright's cup as half empty: they accept that copyright owners should get some measure of control over copies as an incentive to produce creative works, but they would like copyright to extend only as far as necessary to give this incentive, and treat anything more as an encroachment on the general freedom of everyone to write and say as they please.[32]

30. For most developing countries and countries in transition, copyright protection is important as it helps in the development of copyright-based industries, which in turn contribute to overall economic development. One may argue that countries with strong copyright protection such as India, South Korea and the US have robust copyright industries including software, music and film. On the other hand, there are scholars who argue that copyright protection especially in the digital environment creates a barrier to access to information especially teaching and learning materials. However, most developing countries and countries in transition like Kenya, South Africa, Ghana and Nigeria have strong copyright laws that have been updated in the last twenty years taking into account the developments at local, regional and international levels but the man issue if enforcement which affects the growth and development of industries.

§2. Sources – Legislation

I. International Protection of Copyright and Related Rights

31. Transborder use of copyright works necessitated the need to have protection that covered countries beyond the national level. Copyright protection like other IP rights is territorial and if it is not protected in another country, then one cannot enforce the rights abroad. This necessitated the need for multi-lateral agreements

31. For further reading on the history of copyright and author's right, *see* D Burkitt, (2001). Copyright Culture: The History and Cultural Specificity of the Western Model of Copyright. *I.P.Q.* 146–186.
32. Paul Goldstein, (2003) *Copyright's Highway*, Stanford, Stanford University Press p. 10–11.

that provide minimum standard for parties to the treaty. There are several instruments that have been adopted over the years in the field of copyright and related rights.

32. The international treaties provide the general principles for protection and provide for the minimum standards. Each Member State is free to provide for the minimum or make provisions that go beyond the minimum provisions. For instance, several countries provide that copyright protection shall subsist for the life of the author plus seventy years, which is beyond the minimum of life plus fifty years as provided for under the Berne Convention.[33]

A. *The Berne Convention*

33. The Berne Convention for the Protection of Literary and Artistic works was adopted on 9 September 1886 and has been revised several times since taking into account the developments in copyright over the years. The first revision was done in 1908 while the last revision was in Paris in 1971 and is the one in use to date. The 1971 revision followed up on the preferential provisions for developing countries. The main aim of the Berne Convention is to provide, effective and uniform protection for authors in their literary and artistic works. The World Intellectual Property Organisation (WIPO) administers the Berne Convention. The Berne Convention is based on three basic principles, namely the principle of national treatment whereby works originating from a Member State enjoys the same protection as that enjoyed by the nationals in other Berne Member States. The second is the automatic protection of works, and third is the independence of protection of works.

34. Works protected under the Berne Convention include original literary and artistic works and derivative works. Under Article 2, the term 'literary and artistic works' applies to 'every production in the literary, scientific and artistic domain, whatever may be the mode or form of expression.' It is important to note that derivative works, those based on other pre-existing works including translations, adaptations, arrangements of music and other alterations of literary or artistic works will receive the same protection. The adaptation of a literary work into a multimedia work will enjoy the same protection. The translation of a Harry Potter novel to Kiswahili will enjoy same protection of the original work.[34] The protection is conferred on the author and his successors in title.[35] The Convention provides the minimum standards of protection including the rights granted, term of protection, limitations and exceptions as well as other flexibilities.

---

33. The EU, the US, Ghana among others provide for the life of the author plus seventy years while countries like Kenya provide for the minimum which is the life of the author plus fifty years.
34. It is important to note that eligibility of copyright will not be negated by virtue of the fact that the work is an infringing work.
35. Article 2(6).

35. Flexibilities include the appendix to the Berne Convention, which provides specific provisions for developing countries in relation to the right of reproduction and the right of translation for works of foreign origin. The appendix augments the existing exceptions to the author's exclusive rights.[36] Countries regarded as developing countries may under certain conditions, depart from the minimum standards of protection provided for in the Convention.[37] So far, few African countries such as Nigeria have incorporated these provisions in their laws and they are deemed to be cumbersome and less practical to implement.

B. The Rome Convention

36. The International Convention for the Protection of Performers, Producers of Phonograms and Broadcasting Organisations (Rome Convention) was adopted on 26 October 1961. This was to provide for protection of related rights at international level. Protection under the Rome Convention does not in any way interfere with the underlying copyright works. Like the Berne Convention, it provides for the principle of national treatment, sets out the criteria for eligibility for protection, minimum standards of protection, the discretionary regulation of the exercise of rights, exceptions and limitations to the rights and restriction on formalities. The duration under the Rome Convention is twenty years from the end of the year in which the fixation took place. As of November 2015, of the ninety-two Member States to the Rome Convention, only nine are from Africa. This is also reflected in their national laws.

C. Other Special Conventions

37. There are other special conventions administered by the WIPO in the field of related rights and these include the Convention for the Protection of Producers of Phonograms Against Unauthorised Duplication of Their Phonograms (Phonograms Convention) Geneva, October 1971 and The Convention Relating to the Distribution of Programme Carrying Signals Transmitted by Satellite (Satellites Convention) Brussels, May 1974. The main purpose of the two conventions was to protect the producers of phonograms and broadcasting organisations against infringement and unauthorised commercial exploitation of their works.

D. The TRIPS Agreement

38. The Agreement on TRIPS was adopted in Marrakech on 15 April 1994 following the Uruguay Round of multilateral negotiations concluded on 15 December 1993. The TRIPS agreement, unlike the WIPO administered treaties, is binding on all World Trade Organisation (WTO) Member States. The Agreement Incorporates

36. Article 2*bis*, Art. 9(2), Art. 10(2), 10*bis* and Art. 30(2)(b).
37. *WIPO Intellectual Property Handbook: Policy, Law and Practice*, pp. 262–266.

Articles 1–21 of the Berne Convention and its appendix save for Article 6*bis* on moral rights. In addition to the principle of national treatment, it provides for the most favoured nation principle.[38] This means that any advantage, favour, privilege or immunity granted by a Member State to its nationals shall also be accorded without conditions to the nationals of other WTO Member States.

39. TRIPs Agreement provides for the protection of the expression of ideas and not the ideas, procedures and methods of operation or mathematical concepts as such. It also covers the compilations of data and computer programs which may be protected as literary works. The protection of computer programs under copyright was based on the protection of the source code or object code, which is considered a literary work. The Agreement also extends the provisions of the three-step test to all exclusive rights granted under copyright. The exception and limitations to exclusive rights shall be confined to special cases, which do not conflict with normal exploitation of the work and do not unreasonably prejudice the interests of the rights holder.[39]

40. TRIPS recognises the rights of the performing artists, producers of phonograms and broadcasting organisations.[40] It recognises the rights of performers in respect of their unfixed performances including the rights to prevent unauthorised fixation of their unfixed performances and the reproduction of such as fixation. They also have the right to prevent the unauthorised broadcast by wireless means and communication to the public of their live performances. Likewise, producers enjoy the right to authorise or prohibit direct or indirect reproduction of their phonograms.[41] Broadcasting organisations have not been left out and under the Agreement they have the right to prohibit the unauthorised fixation, reproduction of their fixations and the rebroadcasting by wireless means of broadcasts as well as the communication to the public of their broadcasts. It takes cognisance of situations where a country that is a WTO Member State does not grant the rights to the broadcasting organisations, then the right owners in the underlying copyright in the broadcast can have possibility of preventing the said acts.[42] The rental rights provided for under Article 11 of the Agreement shall apply to computer programs shall apply to producers of phonograms as determined by the national law. The term of protection for performers and producers of phonograms is fifty years from the end of the year in which the fixation of the performance was made and twenty years for the Broadcast.[43]

41. Part III of the TRIPS Agreement has specific provisions for the enforcement of IPR. It is notable that the other treaties leave enforcement to be dealt with by domestic legislation and provide no minimum standard. This was addressed in the Agreement especially with the transnational trade in copyright works. Members are

38. Articles 3 and 4.
39. Article 13.
40. Article 14.
41. Article 14(3).
42. Article 14(3).
43. Article 14(5).

required to put in place measures, which offer effective action against infringement of IP and these should be fair and equitable. The remedies include civil and administrative procedures, provisional measures, border measures, and criminal procedures as will be discussed in the chapter on enforcement.

E. WIPO Internet Treaties

42. Advances in technology have had a major impact in the way copyright works are created and disseminated and used. There were several issues that came about due to technological developments that needed to be addressed under the international regime on copyright and related rights. In December 1996, the WIPO Copyright Treaty (WCT) and the WIPO Performances and Phonograms Treaty (WPPT) treaties were adopted. The two treaties sought to address the so-called Digital Agenda. These include the definition of the right of reproduction, transmission on digital networks, limitations and exceptions and storage of works within the digital environment, technological protection measures and rights management information.

1. WIPO Copyright Treaty

43. On the right of reproduction in the digital environment, the Agreed Statements concerning Article 1(4) of the WCT states 'that the reproduction right, as set out in Article 9 of the Berne Convention, and the exceptions permitted thereunder, fully apply in the digital environment, in particular to the use of works in digital form. It is understood that the storage of a protected work in digital form in an electronic medium constitutes a reproduction within the meaning of Article 9 of the Berne Convention.' The issue that arises in the digital environment is whether or not this would be applied in case of social media where the files are shared. Technically, on the reading of this article, reproduction applies even where it is temporary and in any electronic form.

44. There was an agreement as to the transmission of works on the Internet and other similar frameworks should be the object of the exclusive right of authorisation of the author or other copyright owner with the relevant exceptions.[44] Due to the different legal characterisations of digital transmissions, there was need to come up with an amicable solution which ended up being what is known as the 'Umbrella solution' This provided that the act of digital transmission should be described in a neutral form both technologically and legally. The limitations and exceptions were set out in Article 10. There was an agreed statement to clarify the applicability of the Article. The Treaty also provides for protection of technological protection measures and rights management information systems.[45] The Member States are

44. WIPO, *WIPO Intellectual Property Handbook: Policy, Law and Use*, pp. 271–272.
45. *Article 11 and 12 of the WCT.*

required to provide adequate legal protection and effective remedies against circumvention of effective technological protection measures. This also applies to rights management information systems.

45. Other substantive provisions include criteria for eligibility, subject matter and scope of protection, protected rights, duration, exceptions and limitations and enforcement of rights.[46] Like the TRIPS Agreement, the WCT extends the three-step test to all exclusive rights.

2. WIPO Performances and Phonograms Treaty

46. The WPPT was concluded to update the rights of the performers and producers of phonograms under the Rome Convention. However, it is important to note that in general, the application of substantive provisions of the Rome Convention is not an obligation on the contracting parties. There are a few provisions such as those relating to criteria and eligibility, which is included by reference.[47] In addition to the digital agenda as discussed above, the treaty also has substantive provisions in relation to criteria for eligibility, national treatment, rights of the performers including moral rights, rights of producers of phonograms, right remuneration for broadcasting and communication to the public, exceptions and limitations, transferability of rights and duration for protection.

F. The Beijing Treaty

47. WIPO Member States adopted the Beijing Treaty on Audiovisual Performances in June 2012. Protection of audiovisual performances was first addressed in the Rome Convention but there was a need to update the same in line with rights of the performers, and broadcasting organisations. During the discussions leading to the adoption of the WIPO Internet Treaties, WIPO Member States were of the considered opinion that rights in audiovisual performances should be discussed separately. In 2000, a diplomatic conference was convened to adopt the proposed treaty but failed due to differences among WIPO Member States on Article 12; transfer of rights. In 2012, the Diplomatic conference was convened and the Treaty adopted after the Member States came to a compromise of the wording of Article 12 and the relevant agreed statements. The treaty took into account the WIPO development agenda for the benefit of developing countries. Kenya signed the treaty but is yet to ratify it.

---

46. Article 3, Art. 6(1) Art. 9, Art. 10(10) and Art. 14.
47. WIPO, *WIPO Intellectual Property Handbook: Policy Law and Use,* p. 325.

G. The Marrakesh Treaty to Facilitate Access to Published Works for People Who Are Blind, Visually Impaired or Otherwise Print Disabled (WIPO VIP Treaty)

48. One of the most unique treaties adopted by the WIPO Member States is the Marrakesh Treaty to Facilitate Access to Published Works for People who are Blind, Visually Impaired or Otherwise Print Disabled. This is the first WIPO Treaty that has a human rights angle and deals with exceptions and limitations to copyright to allow access for persons who are blind or visually impaired. The Treaty was adopted in 2013 in Marrakesh.[48] Kenya has yet to ratify the treaty but has included the substantive provisions in the proposed amendment to the Act.

II. Copyright Law and Related Rights in Kenya

49. The history of copyright law in Kenya can be traced back to 1897 when the English East Africa Order in Council was passed extending the application of the UK Copyright law substance of English common law, doctrines of equity and the statutes of general application to the then protectorate of Kenya through the reception clause. In 1966, the first Copyright Act was passed by Parliament in Kenya. This Act was revised in 1975 and subsequently amended in 1982, 1989, 1992 and 1995 to provide for changes in copyright especially due to technological advancements and changing international legal norms. Kenya became a party to the Berne Convention in 1993 and had to ensure that the law was compliant with provisions of the Berne Convention Significant amendments included protection of sound recordings and computer programs.

50. As a member of the WTO, Kenya had to ensure that the law was also TRIPs compliant. In 2001, the Copyright Act of 2001 (Now Cap. 130 of the Laws of Kenya) was passed effectively repealing the 1966 Act and took into account the provisions of the TRIPs Agreement, the WPPT and the WCT although it has yet to ratify the two WIPO Internet Treaties the Beijing Treaty for the Protection of Audiovisual performers and the Marrakesh Treaty for to facilitate access to published works for people who are blind, visually impaired or otherwise print disabled. Kenya is a Member of the Berne Convention and as a Member of the WTO is party to the TRIPs Agreement.

51. The Constitution of Kenya of 2010 made significant provisions to ensure that copyright and related rights are protected within the constitutional framework. Article 2(5) of the Constitution provides that the general principles of international law shall apply in Kenya. Article 40(5) provides that the State shall promote and protect IPR of the people of Kenya. This makes copyright protection in Kenya constitutional as copyright is protected like any other property in Kenya.

---

48. As of 9 Sep. 2016, twenty-two Countries had ratified the Treaty which will be coming into force on 30 Sep. 2016.

52. The Kenya Copyright Board (KECOBO), a State Agency under the Office of the Attorney General and Department of Justice administers the Copyright Act in Kenya. It was established under section 3 of the Copyright Act with a mandate to administer and enforce copyright and related rights in Kenya. Its functions include review of legislation, participation in national, regional and international *fora* on copyright and related rights, advise government on matters of copyright, license and supervise collective management organisations, maintain a database, enforce copyright and related rights, training and awareness creation and protection of traditional knowledge (TK).

§3. Subject Matter of Protection

I. Different Categories of Protected Works

53. Copyright protection covers several categories of works, which are usually defined in national laws. Literary works have been subject to copyright protection since the promulgation of the Statute of Anne in 1710. Protected works include works of literature, any works expressed in writing including digital works and original databases. In African countries like Kenya, these cover books, computer programs, magazines, stories, poetic works, scripts, plays, and sheet music, letters and memoranda, lectures and sermons, charts and tables and compilations of data, which are protected regardless of the quality. Blogs, being written works also fall under this category.

54. Section 2 of the Copyright Act Chapter 130 of the Laws of Kenya provides definitions of different types of works covered under copyright. Artistic works include visual arts such as paintings, drawings, etchings, lithographs, woodcuts, engraving and prints, maps and diagrams, works of sculpture, photographs, graphic designs, works of architecture and artistic craftsmanship and works of applied handicraft and industrial design and 3D works. These are also protected regardless of the artistic quality.

55. Musical works are works consisting of music exclusive of the lyrics or performance meant to accompany the music. This covers the sounds that have been arranged in a certain manner to appeal to the listener's emotions and intellect. Mere sound or noise does not qualify to be a musical work.

56. Dramatic works are basically works that are capable of being performed. Cinematographic works are protected under copyright and they cover all audiovisual works such as films, documentaries, television programs. Initially the cinematographic works did not include the audio until the advent of what was then known as 'talking films.' The cinematographic work may or may not include the audio or sound recording but is still protected as such. Published works are also protected under copyright.

57. Related rights include sound recordings, broadcasts and performers rights. Sound recordings were initially treated as musical works but later enjoyed their own protection. These include all forms of recordings from vinyl records to digital files that embody sound recordings. Broadcasts are also protected under copyright though it does not create copyright works but rather communicates the content to a larger audience. Broadcasts are protected due to the substantive investment in the transmission of the content to the audience. This might become more difficult in the digital environment with the content being produced and transmitted over the digital networks by non-traditional broadcasting organisations. Performers are also protected under the Act.

II. Works Excluded of Protection

58. It is important to note that names and titles are not protected as literary works. It is thus possible to have different works with the same name, title of the headline. The law also excludes judicial decisions and written law. Works created by the Government are excluded from copyright protection and these include statutes, judicial decisions, speeches and press releases as well as reports. Ideas, concepts and principles are not protected by copyright. As earlier stated, what is protected is the expression of the idea as one cannot have monopoly over ideas. Works that have not been reduced to a tangible format are not covered by copyright.[49] Public domain works are works that do not fall within the scope of copyright protection either because the owner has renounced the copyright, allowed the use of the works through for instance a creative commons licence or the work was not eligible for copyright protection. Where the works are excluded from copyright protection, users do not require the permission of the authors, for instance, the government in the case of statutes to use the same.

§4. Conditions of protection

I. Formal Requirements

59. Unlike other forms of IP, copyright confers automatically and there are no formalities required for the enjoyment of the same. This is in line with the provisions of Article 5(2) of the Berne Convention. Section 22(3) for a literary, musical or artistic work to be eligible for copyright protection, it must be original and fixed in a material form. A work shall not be ineligible for copyright if the work has been created from an existing work amounting to an infringement of some other work.

---

49. However, in Zimbabwe, the law allows for protection of works under copyright even in cases where this have not been reduced into some tangible form. This was meant to cater for traditional cultural expressions which are no necessarily reduced to material form.

II. Substantive Requirements

A. *Originality*

60. For a work to be eligible for copyright protection, it has to be original, that is, there has to be some skill, labour and judgement in the creation of the work. A work that has been created from an existing work will be deemed to be original. For instance, if one creates a television series from an existing novel, then the series will be deemed to be original as the author has exercised some skill, labour and judgement in creating the television series. In the case of *Alternative Media v. Safaricom* the court held that, the plaintiff's effort was original and that it was not necessary for the plaintiff to prove that the work was uniquely artistic.[50] In the case of *Jiwani v. Going Out Magazine and Another*, the court held in favour of the plaintiff as it found sufficient skill and labour had been expended by the plaintiff by way of formatting, design, collection, photography and development to give it an original character.[51]

61. A work will not be ineligible for copyright protection if it builds upon or draws from an existing work. These are known as derivative works and are eligible for copyright protection. However, the author of the new work has to obtain authority from the original work. It is very common to see creators in the music industry use or sample other people's music to create a new work. A good example is where Pharrell Williams, an American artist was taken to court by the family of the late Marvin Gay for his song 'Blurred lines.' Although the work infringed on the Marvin Gay song 'Got to Give it Up,' it is eligible for copyright protection as a separate work. However, for sampling, he should have obtained the permission of the successors in title. Outright plagiarism of literary work would not pass the test of originality as there is no exercise of skill and judgment as required under copyright.

B. *Fixation*

62. Unlike other IP, copyright confers automatically once it has been reduced into a material format. This includes transient copies in the digital networks. In countries like Zimbabwe, works may be protected even where they are not fixed or reduced to a material format.

C. *Must Not Be Excluded from Protection*

63. There are certain works that may be excluded from copyright protection either expressly by law or through policy decisions. For instance, judicial decisions and statutes may be excluded from copyright cases. In some countries such as the

50. *Alternative Media v. Safaricom* HCCC No. 263 of 2004.
51. *Jiwani v. Going Out Magazine and Another* Civil Suit No. 856 of 2002.

UK, even where a work is original and reduced to material form, copyright protection may be denied if it is deemed to be blasphemous, obscene or immoral and is against public interest.

§5. Ownership

I. The Author (Initial Authorship)

64. An author of a work is the person who creates the work. Under section 2 of the Act, for a literary, artistic or dramatic work, an author is the person who first made or created the work. For audio-visual works, the author is the person whom the arrangements for the making of the audiovisual work were made. This applies to computer programs as well as works generated by computer programs. For sound recordings, the producer is recognised as the author of the work and for films, the producer and the executive director are presumed to be authors of the work. The mere provision of finance does not make a person a producer. The producer is the person who exercises some degree of organisational control over the production of the work. This varies with the legal system. In the civil law countries, the work is taken to be a work of joint authorship of the scriptwriters, those who adopted the work, the creators of the soundtracks, and the person who directs the production.

II. Joint Works/Works Created by Several Persons

65. There are instances where the works may be created by more than one author. In such cases, unless there is an agreement to the contrary, the joint authors have equal rights in work. It is deemed that the contribution is by all the parties save for instances where the contribution can be quantified which is rare. The authors are in the first instance recognised as the co-owners of work. For the rights in the works to be transferred to third parties such as publishers, the joint author have to provide the authorisation. One party cannot purport to act without the permission of the other party or parties. They are recognised as such and the moral and economic rights will confer on all of them. The rights will be valid for the life of the last surviving author plus fifty years.[52]

III. Works Made for Hire

66. The author of the work is presumed to be the owner of the work subject to exceptions as set out by the law. Section 31 of the Copyright Act provides that where the work is created within the course of employment or on commission, the work belongs to the employer or the person who commissioned the work unless there is a contract or agreement to the contrary. The author can sign a contract with

52. In countries like Ghana, US and European Member States, it will be the life of the last surviving author plus 70 years.

the employer or person who commissions the work to retain all or some of the economic rights. The moral rights are not transferred but remain with the author of the work. In the United States, the moral rights are not recognised as such and in other countries like the UK, the author can waive their moral rights. For works created by an employee of the Government or an international organisation, the works will belong to the government or international organisation.

§6. Transfer and Management

I. Assignment or License of Copyright

67. Copyright, like any other moveable property can be transferred by sale, testamentary disposition or licensing. Section 2 of the Copyright Act[53] defines a license as a lawfully granted license permitting the doing of an act controlled by copyright. Acts controlled by copyright include reproducing a protected work, translating or adapting it, distributing the work to the public by way of sale, loan, lease, etc., and communicating and broadcasting of the whole or a substantial part of a protected work.[54] These rights may be licensed out either by the author or owner of the work. The rights to public performance and broadcasting as well as the right of making available may be licensed by a registered collective management organisation to which such rights have been transferred.[55] This means that any person who does any act controlled by copyright without the authorisation of the owner or his licensee or assignee will be infringing under section 35 of the Copyright Act.

68. The transfer should be in writing. This provision was necessary as previously, rights holders, especially in the music industry did not have written agreements and also had a tendency of getting into multiple agreements for the same rights in a particular work. The licences granted may be exclusive on non-exclusive. Licensing and assignment of rights form the basis of collective management of rights. There are those rights that the author/rights holder can exercise individually such as the right sale, but there are those that require collective management such as broadcasting, public performance, reprographic and communication to the public.

69. The Copyright Act recognises exclusive and non-exclusive licenses as two types of licenses.[56] As mentioned above, an exclusive license in copyright is one where a copyright owner transfers one or more of his/her bundle of rights. The owner may transfer part of or the entire bundle of rights to a third party for a specific period of time. This is common in the audio and audiovisual industry as well

53. Cap. 130, Laws of Kenya.
54. Section 26, *Copyright Act*, Cap. 130 of the Laws of Kenya.
55. Section 48(4), *ibid* defines a collecting society as 'an organization which has as its main object, or one of its main objects, the negotiating for the collection and distribution of royalties and the granting of **licenses** in respect of copyright works or performer's rights … ' (emphasis added) *See also Music Copyright Society of Kenya v. Tom Odhiambo Ogowl* [2014] eKLR.
56. *Ibid.*, s. 33.

as the software industry. A good example is the case of proprietary software, where the owner licenses the users to use their software including android applications. For one to access software such as Office for Windows, one has to get a licence from the owner. Software licences are usually non-exclusive.

70. During the subsistence of the licence, the licensee has the same rights as the owner of the rights and is entitled to remuneration as well as legal action when the rights are infringed upon. For instance, in the case of films, where an international company grants a non-exclusive right to a local exhibitor, in Kenya, if the film is infringed by another exhibitor or other unlicensed dealers, then the local exhibitor can take legal action an is entitled to the legal recourse.

71. The licensee under an exclusive license becomes the owner of the transferred right during the term of the exclusivity. The terms and conditions of an exclusive licence are clear and in many cases the licensee cannot transfer the rights to a third party. The licence may be specific to a territory as is the case with film rights.

72. A non-exclusive license is one in which the licensee is granted the right to exercise one or more of the copyright owner's bundle of rights, but the copyright owner can still grant a license to third parties to exercise the same right or rights at the same time, and/or the copyright owner retains authorisation to use the same right(s) that is/are licensed.[57] Software licences are usually non-exclusive.

73. Certain formalities must be observed. Section 33(3) of the Copyright Act provides that no exclusive license shall have effect unless it is in writing and signed by, or on behalf of, the licensor. Under section 33(4), a non-exclusive license may have legal effect if it is either in writing, oral, or can be inferred from the conduct of the parties. It may be revoked at any time. However, where a non-exclusive license is granted by contract, then the license may not be revoked by the licensor or on his behalf except as provided by the contract.

74. Though not expressly stated in the Copyright Act, an exclusive licensee has the power to sub-license unless the contract states otherwise. Section 34 provides for rights of action and remedies for exclusive licensees and sub-licensees, demonstrating that the lawmakers envisaged a situation where the holder of an exclusive license can further sub-license some of the rights licensed to them. Since an exclusive license is granted in writing, and states the rights that have been licensed, the issue of whether or not the licensee may sub-license ought to be expressly stated for the avoidance of confusion. Further regarding sub-licensing, the Act speaks only of sub-licenses in exclusive licenses and at no point mentions sub-licenses in the context of non-exclusive licenses. Written non-exclusive licenses may explicitly grant the right to sub-license.

57. C Tune, *Copyright Licensing Fundamentals*, Understanding the Intellectual Property License 2008. #14730, 3–5

75. Section 34 of the Copyright Act provides for the rights of action and remedies available to exclusive licensees and sub-licensees. Under section 34(1), the licensee or sub-licensee shall be entitled to the same rights of action as though they were assignees of those rights and such rights and remedies shall be concurrent with the rights and remedies of the owner of the copyright. This means that an exclusive licensee or exclusive sub-licensee has the right to institute proceedings to recover such remedies and enforce such rights granted to them. This is qualified, however, by section 34(2), which states that the licensee must give a notice in writing to the owner of the copyright of his intention to institute legal proceedings and the owner may intervene in such proceedings and recover any damages s/he may have suffered.[58]

76. Under collective management of rights, the authors, composers, publishers, producers of sound recordings and performers assign their rights in broadcasting, public performance and making available to the collective management organisations (CMOs) such as the Kenya Association of Music Producers (KAMP), and Performers Rights Society of Kenya (PRiSK). The CMOs subsequently license users such as broadcasting organisations, shopping malls, telecommunication companies to use the works in exchange for a royalty payment. The licences are non-exclusive and help in the collective management of the rights. These are usually issued on an annual basis.

77. In the case of reprographic rights, the authors in the literary, music and visual arts authorise the CMO, in this case Reprographic Rights Organization of Kenya (KOPIKEN), to license the reproduction of their works among users such as libraries, educational institutions, photocopy shops among others. The licensing is also done for digital use of works online.

II. Collective Management

78. Administration of individual rights can be quite difficult especially in cases where there are multiple users such as broadcasting, communication to the public, mechanical reproduction rights and reprographic rights. In order to make the collection of royalties more practical and efficient for both the rights holder and the users (broadcasting organisations, telcos, shopping malls, clubs and other places where the works are publicly performed or made available to the public), the collective management organisations administer the right on behalf of the rights holders. Collective management is the exercise of copyright and related rights by organisations acting in the interest and on behalf of the owners of rights.[59]

79. In Kenya, section 46 of the Copyright Act provides for collective management of rights. In the Music Industry, there are three collective management organisations representing different rights holders. The KAMP represents producers of

58. *Ibid.*, s. 34.
59. *See* WIPO https://www.wipo.int/copyright/en/management/.

sound recordings, Music Copyright Society of Kenya (MCSK) represents composers, authors and publishers while PRiSK represents performers in both the audio and audio-visual sectors. The rights holders assign specific rights to the collective management organisations to administer on their behalf. Where the rights holders do not assign the rights, then the CMOs cannot subsequently collect on their behalf as was held in *John B. Maina v.* Safaricom (2013) eKLR.

80. In August 2015, KAMP, MCSK and PRiSK came to an agreement with Safaricom, to remit royalties collected from the use of their members' works on *Skiza Tunes.* After protracted legal and operational battles, the three organisations, in 2019, agreed to collect their royalties through joint licensing. This was a mandatory requirement by the KECOBO.[60] For reprographic rights, rights holders are represented by the KOPIKEN, which licenses libraries, universities and photocopy shops for the use of works.

81. These collective management organisations are licensed and supervised by the KECOBO to ensure that they execute their mandate effectively and efficiently for the benefit of the members. Other areas that require collective management include visual arts and photography, but relevant collective management organisations are yet to be formed. Rights holders can also manage their rights through various industry organisations.

§7. Scope of Exclusive Rights

82. Copyright protects the expression of an idea and not the idea or concept. Ideas are not protected under copyright as one cannot have a monopoly over an idea and it is notable that creativity often builds upon creativity. For instance, one cannot claim copyright over the concept for a television programme or format but they can claim protection under copyright for various component of the programme namely the script, the fixation of the performance, and the soundtrack. The format will only be protected in as far as it fulfils the criteria for protection. This also brings about the issue of independence of protection; where two people independently create a work, which is the same or similar, they will each enjoy copyright protection in their respective works. In *Faulu Kenya Deposit Taking Micro-Finance Ltd v. Safaricom,* the court held that it was not possible to find a way to attach the plaintiff's concept paper to any of the categories of works eligible for copyright and the infringement claims could thus not hold as it was a concept paper[61]

83. Copyright grants exclusive rights to the author of the works subject to specific exceptions and limitations. The rights granted are economic and moral rights. The author of the works may use the works to the exclusion of all others; the author

---

60. The Music Publishers Association of Kenya (MPAKE) which had been licensed to collect and distribute royalties between 2015 and 2018, did not get the licence for 2019 but KECOBO licensed them to collect the blank tape levy.

61. *Faulu Kenya Deposit Taking Micro-Finance Ltd. v. Safaricom* Civil Case No. 756 of 2012.

or his successors in title may authorise or prohibit third parties from exercising any of the exclusive rights granted by the law. Section 26 of the Act, provides that economic rights that require authorisation from the author include the right of reproduction, distribution, communication to the public, public performance, broadcast, translation and adaptation as well as rental and lending rights.

I. Moral Rights

84. Independent of the economic rights discussed below, the law recognises what are known as the moral rights of the author. The Berne Convention recognises moral rights.[62] These rights are in countries like Kenya deemed inalienable but may be transferred by testamentary disposition at the demise of the author. The moral rights under the Kenyan law include the right to be acknowledged as the author (right of paternity or attribution right) as well as the right to object to any distortion or mutilation of work that may be deemed to be prejudicial to the interests of the author. (right of integrity) For instance, there was a case that was filed by an author against the publisher. In this matter, the author wanted the publisher to withdraw publications which had errors that she had pointed out during the final proofing but the publisher went ahead to publish and issue the book. The book as published would cast doubt as to the academic standing of the author and would thus be prejudicial to her interests. The matter was eventually settled out of court through mediation by the KECOBO.

II. Economic Rights

85. Copyright also grants the authors the exclusive economic rights which include reproduction, distribution, communication to the public, broadcasting, public performance, adaptation and translation. These rights are granted for the life of the author plus fifty years but are subject to exceptions and limitations.

A. *Reproduction Right*

86. The right of reproduction is one of the oldest and most well-known rights granted by copyright. The rights holder has the exclusive right to control the copying of his works by third parties; he can authorise or prohibit the direct or even indirect copying of the work whether permanent, transient or temporary. In the digital environment, the reproduction can be through outright digital copying, surfing of websites, caching, downloads, and the use of social media. For instance, when one

62. Some countries like the Unites States of America do not recognise the moral rights and even under the TRIPS Agreement, they are not mandatory. The EU Member States save for the United Kingdom see moral rights as part and parcel of one's persona and they are inalienable. They cannot be transferred even after the economic rights are transferred. In the United Kingdom, the law allows one to waive their moral rights.

accesses material that is accessed from the memory of a computer, a temporary/transient copy is made. When works are sent via social media, temporary copies are made and this constitutes a reproduction of the work.

87. Rights holders also have the exclusive right to control the distribution of the work in both the digital and non-digital environment. This right becomes more difficult to enforce in the digital environment as there are different distribution channels most of which the rights holder has no control over as was the case in the non-digital environment. It is important to note that the right of distribution is subject to exhaustion upon the first sale of the work. For instance, once an author has sold a book to a publisher, the author has no right to control what the person who has purchased the book does with that particular copy. In addition, there is a right to control hiring or renting of the work especially books and DVDs. The rights holder will also have the exclusive right to import the works.

B. Performing Rights

88. The right of public performance includes recitals and dramatic and musical performances before an audience. This is often referred to as 'performing right.' It is notable that the performing right does not cover artistic works.

C. Translation and Adaptation Rights

89. Translation and adaptation of works also require the authorisation of the rights holder. For instance, for one to translate a book from English to Kiswahili, one has to get authorisation from the author or rights holder. Adaptation involves the modification of a work from one form to another. This could be from a book to a motion picture as was the case with Chimamanda Ngozi Adichie's novel *'Half of a Yellow Sun,'* which was adopted into a motion picture. The resulting works enjoy copyright protection as well.

D. Right of Communication to the Public

90. Communication to the public is a right granted under most copyright laws in Africa. It is defined to include live performances as well as transmission of images, sound or both to the public other than through a broadcast. The right presupposes that the works are communicated from one point to a wider audience as is the case with a live performance. However, with advances in technology, the communication of a work can be from one point to different points enabling the user to access the work at their own time through their preferred devices. The WIPO Copyright Treaties and the WIPO Beijing Treaty took cognisance of this and made a provision for the right of making available by wire or wireless means. This makes it possible for instance for collective management organisations to collect money for the use of works over the Internet by content service providers and telephone companies. It covers individual communications to persons who are part of the public but in their own time and at their own convenience. This right will cover services over the digital networks such as interactive and on demand services such as file sharing systems including social media and Internet transmissions excluding broadcasts.

E. Broadcasting Right

91. The author of a work has the right to authorise or prohibit the broadcast of his works by third parties. If a broadcasting organisation wishes to broadcast a work, they need to get the authority of the rights holder. The work may be broadcast to the public by wire or wireless means. Traditionally, this was done through transmission of programme carrying signals via satellite or cable. It is notable that with the ever-changing technology and digital migration of broadcasting, the right may need to be redefined as the signals can now be intercepted and transmitted via the Internet and other digital networks. Under the Berne Convention, rights holders have the exclusive right to authorise the wireless broadcast as well as diffusion by cable. The rights holders in the digital environment have the right of making available of their works. Convergence of technologies also has had an impact on the way we access and distribute content. With a phone, one can access the Internet, as well as content that is streamed or uploaded online.

F. Droit De Suite

92. The Copyright (Amendment) Act 2017 also seeks to introduce the Artist resale right, which shall be valid as long as the copyright subsists in work. This right is inalienable and cannot be waived. This provision, when enacted, will enable the authors of certain works to benefit each time his work is sold through an art market professional.[63]

§8. Limitations or Exemptions to the Scope of Copyright Protection

93. Exclusive rights discussed above are subject to certain exceptions and limitations. These are meant to provide a balance between the rights of the authors and the interests of the users. Article 9(2) of the Berne Convention states that Member States shall permit the reproduction of literary and artistic works in certain special cases that do not conflict with the normal exploitation of the work and does not unreasonably prejudice the legitimate interests of the author. This is what is known as the three-step test and was incorporated in the TRIPS Agreement Article 13 which extended the three-step test to other rights. These provisions are included in the WPPT, WCT, Beijing Treaty and Marrakesh Treaty.

---

63. Artist's Resale right *see* https://www.gov.uk/guidance/artists-resale-right (last accessed on 18 Apr. 2017).

94. Limitations and exceptions in Kenya are modelled along the provisions of the 1966 Act that borrowed from the UK Copyright and Designs Act of 1956. Section 26 of the Act provides fair dealing and specific exceptions and limitations. Exclusive rights granted for literary, musical and artistic works are subject to the following exceptions:

(a) Exercise of exclusive rights by way of fair-dealing for purposes of scientific research, private use of criticism or review or for news purposes provided the source is acknowledged.
(b) Incidental use of artistic works in a broadcast, broadcasting of a work for systematic instructional activities.
(c) Inclusion of not more than two passages of a literary or a musical work for educational purposes. This is quite restrictive and has an impact on access to teaching and learning materials.
(d) Reproduction of works by the government or public libraries in public interest.
(e) Use of works for judicial proceedings.

95. There are exceptions and limitations that related to computer programs and these are clearly laid out in section 26(3) to (6). Fair dealing does not apply in the case of computer programs. However, a third party may make copies of the program for purposes of correcting errors, creating of a backup copy, testing of the program's suitability and any permitted uses under the licence agreement. Decompilation of the program to allow interoperability falls within permitted uses, but any copies made under these exceptions shall only be used for the purposes outlined above.

96. These exceptions and limitations are deemed to be quite narrowly construed and do not provide for the necessary balance between the rights of the authors and the interests of the users. In order to address this issue, the KECOBO has proposed amendments to the Act to include exceptions and limitations for persons who are blind, visually impaired or otherwise print disabled in line with the provisions of the Marrakesh Treaty, libraries and archives and education and research institutions. The Copyright (Amendment) Bill 2017, has more elaborate exceptions and limitations. It clearly lays out specific exceptions:

- for persons who are blind, visually impaired or otherwise print disabled (section 26C);
- allowing circumvention of technological protection measures for persons who would benefit from exceptions and limitations under the Act (section 26B);
- exceptions and limitations for computer programs (section 26A);
- the second schedule sets out the general exceptions and limitations, exceptions as they relate to educational institutions, libraries and archives as well as in the case of broadcasting.

97. The amendments seek to provide further clarity on exceptions and limitations especially as they relate to computer programs and broadcasting. They also provide for more expansive exceptions and limitations to create a balance between the rights of the authors/owners and the enable access by users without infringement.

§9. Duration of Protection

98. Protection under copyright is limited. The minimum term of protection for copyright is the life of the author plus fifty years, but there are countries like Members of the European Union (EU) and the United States who have increased the term for the life of the author plus seventy years. Interestingly, Jamaica has the longest term of protection, which is calculated as life plus ninety years! For sound recordings, performances and broadcasts, the term is calculated as fifty years from the end of the year when the work was first published. The extension of the term of protection has generated a lot of debate at the national, regional and international level. This is more so in the case of software and more recently mobile applications, which have a limited lifespan. In the case of anonymous works, the term of protection will be calculated from the end of the year of the first publication of the work.

99. In Kenya, section 23(2) the term of protection is the life of the author plus fifty years in the case of literary, musical and artistic works. Where joint authors create the work, copyright protection will be the life of the last surviving author plus fifty years. For audiovisual works and photographs, protection is calculated for fifty years from the end of the year when the work was first published. Sound recordings and broadcasts are also protected for fifty years from the end of the year when the work was first recorded or when the broadcast took place. Moral rights for literary, artistic and musical works and for performers subsist in perpetuity. They are not transferrable.

100. Works that do not enjoy copyright protection are deemed to be in public domain. Under section 45 of the Copyright Act Cap. 130 of the Laws of Kenya, works considered to be in public domain are:

(a) works whose term of protection has expired;
(b) works where the owner has declared the same to be in public domain by renouncing their rights in them in writing which has to be made public;
(c) foreign works that do not enjoy copyright protection in Kenya.

101. When a work is in public domain, third parties may use the works and also come up with new works. Public domain is one of the flexibilities offered under copyright law to ensure access to works. Interestingly, in Kenya the law requires one to pay a certain fee to the Attorney General, but they may use the work without any restriction.

§10. NEIGHBOURING RIGHTS

102. Section 28 of Cap. 130 provides producers of sound recordings with exclusive rights to control the direct or indirect reproduction of the sound recording in any manner or form, distribution of the works, importation into the country and communication to the public or the broadcasting of a sound recording in part or in whole. The rights are similar to those granted for literary, musical and artistic works.

103. Broadcasts also enjoy protection under section 29 of the Copyright Act. The owner of the broadcast has the exclusive right to control fixation, rebroadcast, and communication to the public of part of or the whole broadcast. This does not in any way prejudice the interests of the rights holders in the underlying copyright works where applicable.

104. Performer's rights were included in the Act in section 30. The Act provides for exclusive rights as well as equitable remuneration under section 30A. The exclusive rights granted under section 30 include broadcast of the live performance, communication to the public of a performance under specific circumstances, make a fixation of a previously unfixed performance and reproduction and rental of a fixed performance. The provisions cover both audio and audiovisual performers. Moral rights of the performer are covered under section 33 of the Act. Unlike copyright, the protection is for a period of fifty years from the end of the year in which the performance took place.

105. In addition to exclusive rights granted under the Copyright Act, Performers and producers of sound recordings have the right to equitable remuneration for the use of sound recordings and audiovisual works by third parties under section 30A. The right forms the basis of collection of royalties for the use of works by third parties such as phone companies and content service providers. This is because the Act recognises that sound recordings and fixations of performances that have been made available to members of the public in such a way that they may access them individually and at a time chosen by them as publication for commercial purposes. This takes into account use of works by third parties over digital networks. The Act provides specific exceptions and limitations in relation to related rights.

106. The enactment of section 30(A) of the Act enabled producers of sound recordings and performers to get equitable remuneration, which was paid through the collective management organisations namely KAMP and PRiSK. This provision has however been subject to constitutional review cases both at the Constitutional Court and the High Court.

§11. Infringement and Remedies

I. Legal Provisions

107. When a third party exercises the exclusive rights without the authority of the rights holders and not within the permitted uses under exceptions and limitation, it amounts to infringement of copyright and related rights. Infringement of the work may be direct or indirect, in whole or a substantial part of the work. This is known as primary infringement and is covered under section 35(1) and (2) of the Copyright Act. Secondary infringement on the other hand covers unauthorised acts that aid and abet the primary infringer. These include circumvention of technological protection measures, manufacture and or distribution of devices that are primarily designed to circumvent technological protection measures or to create infringing works. The main difference between primary and secondary infringement is that in the former where the focus is on those directly involved in the infringement while the latter is concerned with dealing in the commercial context through dealing with infringing copies, enabling such copying and facilitate the public performance of a work.

108. In Kenya, section 35 of the Act provides for infringement which gives rise to civil liability while section 38 creates offences in relation to the unauthorised use of copyright and related rights. Remedies available under section 35(4) are relief by way of damages, delivery up to the plaintiff of any article by the defendant that is deemed infringing by the Court, injunctions and reasonable royalty. Where the Court is not satisfied that the relief will be effective, it may award additional damages which it considers appropriate in the circumstances. Section 35(10) provides for the presumption of ownership unless the contrary is proved. In *Alternative Media v. Safaricom,*[64] the court held that the defendant had infringed on the plaintiff's copyright and granted an interlocutory injunction against the defendant while awarding the plaintiff KES 100,000 in damages.

109. Anton Piller Orders have proved to be essential in preservation of evidence prior to commencement of infringement actions. Section 37 provides that where a person has prima facie evidence that his rights have been infringed, then he can apply to the court for Anton Piller Orders. These measures secure the preservation of evidence in suspected copyright infringement cases and the orders are granted ex parte. In *Microsoft Corporation v. Mitsumi Computer Garage Ltd,*[65] the court held that the plaintiff had failed to show that all the requirements for the *Anton Piller* Orders had been satisfied and declined to grant the orders.

110. The law provides defences for infringement. Where infringement is proved or a party admits to committing the infringement but shows that at the time of committing the infringement, he had no idea that copyright subsisted in the work, the plaintiff shall not be entitled to any damages against the defendant but is entitled to

64. *Alternative Media v. Safaricom* (HCCC No. 263 of 2004).
65. *Microsoft Corporation v. Mitsumi Garage Ltd.* (2001) 1 EA 127.

other relief. This defence has successfully been used in a number of infringement cases where the defendant(s) proved that they had no idea of the existence of copyright in the work.

111. Offences created under section 39 of the Copyright Act include making for sale or hire, selling, or distributing, importing, infringing copies or making or possessing a contrivance for making infringing copies and Illegal/unauthorised public performance of a copyright-protected work. The law provides that the person shall be guilty of an offence unless they can prove that they acted in good faith or had no reasonable grounds to believe that copyright infringement would occur. This defence has also been used in several criminal infringement cases but in many cases, it is difficult to prove.

112. The fines laid out by the law range from a maximum of KES 100,000 or a custodial term of two years, to KES 8,000,000 or a maximum custodial sentence of ten years or both. So far, the highest fine awarded by the Courts in Kenya for copyright infringement is KES 400,000 and a custodial term of six months. The rights holders argue that the fines, which were set in 2001 are not punitive or deterrent and need to be revised to curb the increasing levels of commercial copyright infringement in Kenya. The Government, through the KECOBO, in consultation with stakeholders have proposed amendments to the law which will see the fines pegged on the marker cost per unit, multiplied by the number of infringing copies and the specific unit.

113. The fines as laid out in the law are seen to be none punitive and non-deterrent as first, they were set out in 2001 and have not been revised since, and secondly, since the law provides for the maximum, the courts are at liberty to decide what fines they should give. In most cases, since they do not view copyright infringement as a serious offence, they tend to issue very low fines. The Copyright (Amendment) Bill 2017 seeks to cure this anomaly be providing for fines based on the number of works infringed and the market value of the works. The fine will either be (a) ten times the market value of the works infringed or (b) KES 2,000 per infringing copy, whichever is higher. This is meant to be punitive and deterrent.

114. Infringement of moral rights occurs where a third party fails to recognise the author of the work as such or uses the work in a manner that is prejudicial to the interests of the rights holder such as using a gospel track for the promotion of an alcoholic beverage. Recently, there was a case that was brought to the KECOBO where the author of a book, who is also a university professor was seeking legal recourse against the publishers for publishing a book with factual errors that had been corrected by the author and the corrections not incorporated. Although the case was settled out of court, it was evident that the moral rights of the author had been infringed and the publisher agreed to recall all the publications for destruction including the printing plates and proofs.

II. Cases

A. Alternative Media v. Safaricom (HCCC No. 263 of 2004) [2005] eKLR

115. The plaintiff, in the business of advertising graphic designing and media communication solution, sued the defendant claiming copyright infringement on the plaintiff's design which he claims authorship and ownership. The design was a campaign against the spread of HIV/AIDS and had been submitted to the defendant as a proposal.[66] The plaintiff submitted to the court that the defendant had declined the proposal but later used the said design on the same type of scratch cards for a similar campaign programme. In light of the above facts the plaintiff sought an injunctive order against the defendant for the immediate barring of further distribution of the scratch cards.

Issues

- Ownership of the work.
- Infringement by the defendant.
- Whether or not the plaintiff is eligible to be granted an interlocutory injunction against the defendant.
- Whether or not the plaintiff is eligible for any other damages.

Court Decision

116. On ownership, the court held that the defendant did not contest that the plaintiff came up with the design, but merely that the work was not uniquely artistic. The court held it was not necessary to prove the above and that the plaintiff was an author within the definition of authorship as per section 2(1) of the copyright act and that the totality of the plaintiff's effort was original and the plaintiff was the owner of the design.

117. Court held that the defendant infringed the plaintiff's copyright. The court defined copyright infringement as the translation or the adaptation of the copyright work. The submission by the defendant that the work was hugely different does not prove that the defendant had not infringed, the infringement was a conscious infringement with reference to the exposure the defendant had of the work (the proposal) of the plaintiff.

118. The plaintiff was granted an interlocutory injunction limited to offending artwork. However, the court held that, the plaintiff failed to prove that had the defendant not utilised the design the defendant would have failed to make sales, as such the court only awarded the plaintiff general damages of KES 100,000.

---

66. http://cipit.org/index.php/alternative-media-ltd-v-safaricom-media-lt 2, *Ibid.*

B. John Boniface Maina v. Safaricom Limited & 4 Others (Interactive Media Services Ltd (1st Third Party) Liberty Afrika Technologies Ltd (2nd Third Party) MCSK (3rd Third Party) Cellulant (Kenya) Ltd (4th Third Party)) [2010] Civil suit 808 of 2010

119. Prior to this suit, the plaintiff had brought another application to the court against the defendant claiming copyright infringement for the same works.

120. The plaintiff is a musician/recording artist, authorised the first third party to collect mechanical royalties for all his musical works. The plaintiff claimed that the defendants and the four third parties had infringed his copyright over popular Gikuyu songs, by assigning those rights to the first and second third parties. The plaintiff also claims copyright infringement by the defendant for continued inclusion, reproduction and distribution of his musical works in the *Skiza tunes sales* without the plaintiff's authorisation.

Issues

- Had the plaintiff transferred his rights to the third party?
- Was the defendant still infringing on the plaintiff's work?
- Whether or not the plaintiff is eligible to be granted Anton Piller orders against the defendant and the third parties to seize the offending material?
- Whether the plaintiff is eligible to be granted an injunction against the defendant from further distribution of the offending material?

Court Decision

121. On the first issue, the court was of the opinion that the plaintiff had not transferred his rights or authorised the third party (Music Society of Kenya) to transfer his rights to redistribute or any such rights to any third parties. The court stated that it was clear that the plaintiff was just but a bystander in the conflict between the defendant and the third party.

122. On the second issue, the court was satisfied that the defendant even after claiming to have purged all musical works of the plaintiff from the catalogue, was still using the catalogue of the plaintiff's music and granted the plaintiff limited Anton Piller orders.

123. The Court granted an injunction to the plaintiff as requested.

C. Faulu Kenya Deposit Taking Micro-finance Ltd v. Safaricom Ltd (Civil Case No. 756 of 2012) [2012] eKLR

124. The plaintiff had developed a cash advance system that was to be beneficial to the mobile phone platform and operated on the same. The plaintiff sent the proposal with a concept paper outlining the working of the system to the defendant for a joint venture on its M-Pesa platform. The plaintiff included a non-disclosure agreement, which was signed 12 April 2012. The defendant, however, proceeded to partner with another party (Commercial Bank of Kenya) and launched a cash advance system, which the plaintiff claimed to be similar to that which had been outlined in his concept paper. However the memorandum of understanding signed between Safaricom and Commercial Bank of Kenya is dated 4 April 2012.

Issues

- Was there a copyright in the concept paper?
- Did the plaintiff own the copyright?

Court Decision

125. The court held that try as it may, it failed to find a way to attach the plaintiff's concept paper into any of the categories of works eligible for copyright, the court also stated that the plaintiff had failed to register the advance system under patent and as such was not an owner of utility model or industrial design.

126. The court held that the plaintiff had failed to establish a prima facie case that they had copyright in the concept and the product described in the concept paper and therefore failed to prove infringement of its copyright. The court noted that it had limited jurisdiction in the matter and the matter should be re-directed to the industrial court which has unlimited jurisdiction on such matters.

D. Music Copyright of Kenya v. Parklands Shade Hotel (Civil Case No. 1458 of 2000)

127. The plaintiff filed a suit against the defendant seeking an injunction restraining the defendant from public performance of music whether recorded or live in its premises without paying royalties. The defendant however was of the view that the plaintiff was not the sole licensing body of copyright works, that there was no evidence that the musicians had assigned their rights to the plaintiff and that they had freely negotiated and entered into contracts with the live band performing and whose services it paid for directly. The plaintiff sought injunction to retrain the defendant from playing any recorded or live music of the rights holders.

Issues

- Ownership of the music.
- Status of the plaintiff as a collective management society.
- Infringement of copyright by the defendant.
- Whether or not the plaintiff is eligible to be granted an injunction to restrain Klub House from playing the music without license.

- Whether or not the plaintiff was eligible to be granted damages for the infringement of copyright and conversion together with costs and interest.

Court Decision

128. The court declined to grant the plaintiff the injunction sought as it was not the sole licensing authority to enforce the rights and that the plaintiff failed to establish a prima facie case with a probability of success and that the defendant would suffer irreparable damages should the order sought to be granted.

E. Parity Information Systems v. Vista Solution and 2 Others [2012] eKLR

129. The plaintiff created six software systems and claimed copyright infringement by the defendant, the defendant however was adamant that the nature of the systems were such that they allowed third party to use the tools of the system in developing software applications. The defendant also had a certificate of copyright as he had registered the software earlier than the plaintiff. The defendant sought interlocutory orders including the Anton Piller Order.

Issues

- Whether the injunctive order should be issued against the defendant.

Court Decision

130. Interlocutory injunction was denied to the plaintiff as the court was of the opinion that the plaintiff failed to satisfy the three principles of an interlocutory injunction. The court was of the considered opinion that the plaintiff was unlikely to suffer any irreparable damage. The defendant was however ordered to keep an account of all transactions in relation to its vista management information systems (subject of the suit).

F. Njeri Wangari and Anor v. Oxford University Press (Civil Case No. 866 of 2010) [2012] eKLR

131. The plaintiff alleged that the defendant infringed on her poem 'Their Eyes' in its publication 'Mines and Mind Fields MY SPOKEN WORDS' by copying the poem in its publication 'Counterpoint and Other Poems' without due authorisation from the plaintiff.

Issues

– Whether or not the defendant had infringed plaintiff's copyrights in the works counterpoint and other poems.

Court Decision

132. Authorship of the works was not in question. It was accepted by both the plaintiffs and the defendant that the first plaintiff was the author. The Court held that the second plaintiff failed to prove infringement as the evidence adduced failed to establish a connection between the infringing publication and the works which were subject to the suit. There was no agreement that was produced by the plaintiffs that relate to the works 'mines and mine fields' MY SPOKEN WORDS but rather 'FADING FACES'. It was not clear whether they were one and the same works.

133. It must be noted that it was the second plaintiff's application against the defendant that was proved to be unmeritorious, and since the claim by the plaintiff was intertwined, on the issue of copyright, then both had to be dismissed.

G. Nevin jiwan t-a Go Places Publishing v. Yellow Pages Publishing and Marketing Limited (Civil Case No. 1178 of 2006)

134. The plaintiff, proprietor of Go Places Publishing Magazine, claimed the defendant (a directory magazine) infringed on its copyright by publishing photographs and articles which are the plaintiff's original works. The defendant however was adamant that the infringing works had indeed been provided by the plaintiff and had already been printed and ready for distribution. The plaintiff sought injunctive orders to retrain the defendant from publishing the infringing works.

Issues

– Whether or not the defendant had committed copyright infringement.

Court Decision

135. The Court found that the husband of the plaintiff had worked for the defendant's company, and only brought the suit after his tenure. It was not contested that while he served as the Managing Director of the Defendant Company, it was he who had introduced and approved the now disputed copyrighted material into the defendant's publication programme. It was seen to be impossible and indeed absurd by the court for the said Mansoor Babu Jiwani to sue for IPR of the same said publication through his wife. The application by the plaintiff was dismissed on the grounds of non-disclosure of material facts, the learned judge invoked the equitable principle that '… any party who moves the court for an equitable remedy must first address himself to vital disclosures, otherwise such a party does not come with clean hands and would be held disentitled to equitable remedies ... ' The plaintiff did not disclose the fact that her husband was formerly the managing director at the defendant's company. The court found that the suit was as a result of a family fall-out which involved the plaintiff and the defendant.

H. Jiwani v. Going Out Magazine & Another (Civil Suit No. 856 of 2002)

136. The plaintiff claimed copyright infringement of certain photographs that appeared in the defendant's magazine. The plaintiff's claims were twofold: (i) that the defendant had infringed the plaintiff's copyright in Go Places Magazine and Go Places Restaurant Guide, (ii) as a consequence of the infringement, has caused the plaintiff to suffer losses. Hence the plaintiff's prayers for an injunction order against the defendant, from further publishing and distributing the offending articles and infringing on the plaintiffs copyright to all the photographs designs and artwork.

137. Both parties had been granted leave to file their respective affidavits; however, the defendant failed to file the replying affidavit in the stipulated time. However the defendants argued that the first affidavit was valid as it had not been found defective by the court.

Issues

- Originality of the works in question.
- Copyright infringement by the defendant.
- Relief available.

Court Decision

138. The court held that it did not have powers to extend the time limit by the consent of the litigants however unfair the time limitation might turn out to be. It was only a subsequent consent by the parties could enlarge such time.

139. On whether the plaintiff had established a prima facie case, as there was sufficient skill and labour by way design, formatting, collection, photography and development. The Court held in favour of the plaintiff as it found that the defendant's work a copied and reproduced from the plaintiff's work including the errors and granted the plaintiff an interim prohibitive injunction.

I. Uganda Performing Rights Society Ltd v. Mukubira [2004] 1 EA 343

140. The applicant was the sole assignee of the copyrights in the musical works of Afrigo Band. As a result of the assignment, the applicant had duly assumed the executive rights including control of the distribution of the music rights, public performance for payment and broadcasting. Pursuant to the above, the Applicant filed for a permanent injunction order against the Defendant and damages for copyright infringement and conversion.

Issue

- Whether the court was at liberty in light of the submitted facts to order for Anton Piller Orders against the Defendant (search and seizure order).

Court Decision

141. The court held that an Anton Piller order could only be granted ex parte if the applicant satisfied the following conditions:

(i) that there is in existence a very strong prima facie case;
(ii) that the actual or potential damage is very serious for the applicant;
(iii) that there is clear evidence that the Respondents have in their possession the incriminating evidence; and
(iv) that there is a real possibility that the Respondents would destroy the offending material before any application inter-parties is made.

142. The court granted the Anton Piller orders.

J. Microsoft Corporation v. Mitsumi Computer Garage Ltd [2001] 1 EA 127

143. The plaintiff instituted a suit against the defendant for alleged infringement of its IPR. Simultaneously with the filing of the suit, the plaintiff, ex parte, under a certificate of urgency moved to court for an *Anton Piller* order and prohibitory injunction against the first defendant. The court granted the plaintiff the orders (on the establishment by the plaintiff a prima facie *case* on copyright infringement by the defendant). The court also granted an interim order restraining the first defendant from infringing the copyright in any of its computer software programs by selling, hiring or distributing its pirated computer software programs. However, on the same day the interim orders were granted, the respondent, went to the first defendant's premises and confiscated fifteen computers in purported execution of the order.

Issues

- Whether or not the court should set aside all orders obtained by the plaintiff as a result of use of the wrong procedure.
- Whether or not a prima facie case had been set out for the grant of Anton Piller orders.

Court Decision

144. It was held that procedural lapses should not be invoked to defeat applications unless the lapse was within the jurisdiction of the court or caused substantial prejudice to the adverse party.

145. It was held that nothing had been adduced in court to show that all the requirements for Anton Piller Orders had been satisfied as the affidavit relied on did not touch on the applicant.

K. Cellulant Kenya Ltd v. MCSK (Civil Case No. 154 of 2009) [2009] eKLR

146. Plaintiff was in the business of mobile phone value-added services of musical and artistic works such as phone ringtones, logos and pictures. The plaintiff entered into various mobile content distribution agreements with musicians for different songs. A dispute arose when the plaintiff stopped paying the defendant royalties after it had entered into individual agreements with the artists. The defendant then proceeded to raid the premises of the plaintiff and seized plaintiff's computers on allegations that the plaintiff had breached the copyright of its members.

147. The plaintiff moved to court for an interlocutory injunction, to restrain the defendant or agents.

Issues

- What are the type of rights exist and which are applicable?
- Ownership and transfer of rights.
- Payment of royalties to the Defendant.
- Whether the plaintiff has established a prima facie case to warrant the granting of the interlocutory & mandatory injunctions.

Court Decision

148. On the first issue, the Court held that in this particular case there were two types of copyright that needed to be distinguished, the first being copyright of the author that arises from fixation (as defined in section 2 of the Copyright Act 2001), and copyright that accrues to the author from its communication to the public by public performance. The court stated that it was evident that the plaintiff had confused the two.

149. The court asserted that indeed, as granted by the Copyright Act, the defendant as the collecting society had authority to deal with plaintiff on behalf of its members regardless of the individual agreements.

150. In addition to the above, there was no documentary evidence showing the payments made to the different artists. It was thus apparent that the plaintiff was exploiting the artists and therefore infringing on copyright. He was found liable to pay the accrued royalties to the defendant.

151. However, the court found that there was no legal justification for the defendant to confiscate the plaintiff's computers and thus the plaintiff was granted an injunction to restrain the defendant and any of its employees or agents from going to the plaintiff's premises.

L. Albert Gacheru Kiarie t/a Wamaititu Productions v. Simon Muiruri Kirehu t/a One Stop Music Store (Civil Case 566 of 2003) [2008] eKLR

152. The plaintiff claimed copyright infringement of some of his music recordings, which the defendant reproduced without his permission into CDs, from the plaintiff's cassettes. The plaintiff had acquired the copyright by transfer from the artist Jane Nyambura Kinyua. The rights transferred included, right to produce/ reproduce in any form & can damage the titles of any songs if need be without reference to any person. The defendant however also claimed to have an agreement with the composers.

Issues

- Ownership of Copyright by the plaintiff.
- Copyright infringement by defendant.
- Whether or not the plaintiff is eligible for the order of an injunction in respect of listed and sale of CDs.
- Whether or not the plaintiff is eligible for any special or general damages.

Court Decision

153. With regard to the first issue, it was held that the plaintiff owned the copyright. The court stated that once a copyright is transferred, it becomes of the transferee. Therefore, the defendant's argument that he had entered into similar agreement with the musician was invalid as the rights had already been transferred to the plaintiff.

154. The court held that the defendant infringed on the copyright when transferred the music from the cassettes and reproduces it in CDs, well aware from where they had originated from, as the cassettes carried sufficient information to indicate the producer of the cassettes.

155. The court reaffirmed and upheld the injunctive order that had been issued earlier. However, the court was unsure as to the amount of damages to be awarded to the plaintiff and ordered an inquiry as to the amount of damages.

M. Dedan Maina Warui & Another v. Safaricom Limited. (Misc. Civil Application No. 292 of 2013) [2014] eKLR

156. Plaintiff claimed copyright infringement in his creation 'Med Dispenser' an electronic medical prescription. Plaintiff alleged that he proposed a Joint Venture to the defendant, through its employees and furnished them with detailed information about the product. The plaintiff and the defendant after the completion of the development of the product, signed a non-disclosure agreement. However after the lapse of a certain period of time, the defendant launched 'Safaricom Health Presence' a product, which the plaintiff claimed was similar to his creation the 'Med Dispenser'. The defendant however claimed that the two products were not the same, as the product that it had launched was a video conferencing doctor-patient solution and not mobile telephony. The defendant also claimed that the product launched did not incorporate any ideas from the plaintiff's concept paper but from Cisco Health Presence, which was currently in the public domain. The defendant also submitted the defence that copyright only protects the expression of an idea and not the idea itself.

Issues

- Whether or not the plaintiff has ownership in the copyright to the innovation.
- Whether or not there was copyright infringement.
- Whether or not the plaintiff is eligible for a temporary injunction.

Court Decision

157. On the first issue, it was clear that the plaintiff was the author of the concept paper and as such had copyright in it. The court held however that it was not clear from the plaintiff's submissions, whether the plaintiff was seeking orders based on infringement of the idea of 'Med Dispenser' or the concept paper. That indeed the concept paper was entitled to a copyright as it had been reduced to writing and fixed in writing form, which brings it within the rights of copyright law.

158. On the issue of whether the defendant utilised the data from the creation of the plaintiff therefore infringing on copyright on the information from the 'Cisco Health Presence' the court opined that it was very plausible that two independent parties come up with the same idea but utilised different aspects of technology, and that the plaintiff failed to adduce prima facie evidence to the effect that the defendant relied on the concept paper in the creation of the 'Safaricom Health Presence'.

159. As such the plaintiff was found not eligible for the injunction orders sought, and the application ruled defeated. However the court held that the matter should be set down in hearing on a priority basis, as substantive issues on copyright need to be made clear in the law.

N. Macmillan Kenya Publishers v. Mount Kenya Sundries Ltd (Civil Case No. 2503 of 1995) [2015] eKLR

160. The plaintiff claimed copyright infringement of its maps 'Kenya Tourist Map' later called 'Kenya Travellers Map' by the defendant. The defendant's maps were similar to those of the plaintiff's save for changes. The defendant made a counter-claim that the plaintiff had no *locus standi* and was precluded from lodging the suit as it was barred from the doctrine of laches.

Issues

- Whether or not the plaintiff had ownership rights in the subject matter.
- Whether or not the plaintiff had locus standi in the suit and had locus standi to lodge the suit.
- Whether or not the plaintiff was eligible to be granted an injunctive order.
- Whether or not the plaintiff is eligible for damages.

Court Decision

161. The court held that the plaintiff was the original creator and as such had ownership rights of the map and therefore had locus standi to lodge the suit. The plaintiff therefore was granted an injunction restraining the defendant from selling or offering for sale. An enquiry was ordered as to the amount of damages the plaintiff was eligible for.

O. Elijah Mira alias Elijah Miller v. Interactive Media Services (Civil Suit 974 of 2006) [2007] eKLR

162. The plaintiff claimed to be the owner of the song '*Neguthondeka Njira*'. He discovered that the defendant was selling ringtones that involved the same song infringing on the plaintiff's copyright. The plaintiff sought injunctive orders plus costs of the application pending the hearing and determination of the main suit.

Issues

- Whether the plaintiff was the owner of the artistic work.
- Whether the defendant infringed on the plaintiff's copyright.
- Whether the plaintiff was eligible for injunctive orders.

Court Decision

163. The defendant did not file a response to the application; therefore, the court granted the applicant the prayers as sought.

P. Anne Nang'unda kukali v. Mary Ogola & University of Nairobi (Civil Suit No. 94 of 2010) [2010] eKLR

164. In June 2009, the first respondent submitted to the second respondent a research proposal for a degree of masters in Arts in Project Planning and Management the same material that the applicant had presented to Maseno University for the degree of Master's in Education. The first respondent had received the work in question from the applicant's friend. The first respondent however purported that the work in question was her original work, a fact that the applicant claimed the first respondent knew to be untrue.

Issue

- Whether or not the first respondent infringed on the copyright of the applicant.

Court Decision

165. The court held that indeed the first respondent had infringed on the applicant's copyright by copying almost the entire content of the applicant's research work, which the respondent had been privy to through a friend.

166. As such the applicant was awarded an injunctive order restraining the second defendant from including the first respondent from the graduating list. The applicant was also awarded the order restraining the second respondent from awarding the first respondent a degree certificate.

§12. Copyright in the Digital Environment

I. Introduction

167. Over the years, copyright often plays catch up to advances in technology. Copyright law is versatile and several developments are continuously incorporated into the law or the law interpreted to include these developments. However, copyright in the digital environment and in particular the Internet has continued to face challenges. With digitisation, convergence of technologies namely broadcasting, telecommunications and computers, and the Internet, the way we create, reproduce an, distribute, disseminate, access and store copyright works has changed. It is easier to reproduce perfect copies of a work and disseminate to third parties all over the world in real time, on different platforms, as long as they have access to Internet. It has become harder for the rights holder to control access and use of works. These developments have created challenges as well as opportunities in management, administration and enforcement of copyright and related rights.

168. There are several scholars who believe that this is the end of copyright as we know it but as stated earlier, copyright continues with a few adjustments and changes to incorporate ever-changing technologies. At the International level, several attempts have been made to update international norms to include 'digital copyright'. The WIPO Internet Treaties came up with provisions for the 'digital agenda'.

(a) Storage and reproduction extend to the activities in the digital environment as was clearly stated in the Agreed Statement in line with provisions of Article 9 of the Berne Convention.
(b) Transmission on digital networks; Member States came up with what is known as the 'Umbrella Solution which extends the right of communication to the public to all categories of works including interactive systems and is technologically neutral to take into account any new developments. Article 8 of the WCT and Articles 10 and 14 of the WPPT, and Article 10 of the Beijing Treaty provide for the right of making available. The provision allows Member States to apply the right of making available through the right of communication to the public or other rights such as distribution of a combination of both. In Kenya, the right of making available is currently availed through the right of communication to the public for use of works in the digital environment. This, as discussed earlier, forms the basis of collective management of rights in the digital environment.
(c) Limitations and exceptions in the Digital Environment may be extended to the digital environment and Member States are free to introduce additional exceptions and limitations. The Marrakesh Treaty to facilitate access to published works by visually impaired persons and persons with print disabilities provides access through exceptions and limitations to address what is known as the 'book famine' by beneficiaries of the Treaty. As stated earlier, Kenya is in the process of incorporating the provisions of the Treaty in its copyright law.
(d) Technological protection measures and rights management information. Management of rights in the digital environment may require additional measures beyond copyright. Rights holders often employ technological protection measures such as passwords, encryption, digital signatures among others. Article 11, Article 18 and Article 15 of the WCT, WPPT and Beijing Treaty, respectively, require the Member States to make adequate legal provisions and provide effective legal remedies against the circumvention of technological protection measures used by the rights holders. In Kenya, section 37(3) makes it illegal for one to circumvent technological protection measures, manufacture or distribute devices that can be used to circumvent technological protection measures. These include illegal decoders, and machines capable of decrypting encrypted signals.

    Article 12 of WCT, Article 19 of WPPT and Article 16 of Beijing Treaty require Member States to make legal provisions for protection of rights management systems. These provisions are found in section 35(3) of the Copyright Act which makes it an infringement for one to remove or alter any electronic rights management information or distribute, import or broadcast works as well as make them available where the rights management systems have been removed or altered without the authority of the rights holder. Protection of technological protection measures and rights management systems are crucial in management and enforcement of rights in the digital environment.

In Kenya, the current provision in the Act does not make exceptions in case these are removed or altered by persons who would otherwise have access under exceptions and limitations within the Copyright Act. This is an omission that has been addressed in the Copyright (Amendment) Bill 2017 to ensure access to knowledge for beneficiaries of exceptions and limitations.

(e) Right to remuneration for broadcasting and communication to the public is covered by Article 15 of WPPT and Article 11 of the Beijing Treaty and is also known as the right to equitable remuneration. This is provided for in section 30A of the Copyright Act.

II. Copyright Issues to Consider in the Digital Environment

169. As stated earlier, the Internet has brought up several issues in relation to the creation, dissemination, access and use of copyright-protected works. Reproduction is no longer a simple issue as it includes both permanent and transient copies. For instance, when one streams a movie online, the act of streaming requires one to visit the website to access the content. This contrasts with downloads where copies are actually made and stored in one's device. Many streaming services especially for music and movies for not make their material available for downloading.[67] The use of various programs offered on the Internet to facilitate downloads of streaming services is illegal as they use circumvention technologies. New media and forms of access and communication continually challenge the right of the author/ rights holder to control the reproduction and distribution of their works online and in other digital networks.

170. Even with more content being accessed online, the authors and rights holders do not necessarily get adequately compensated for the use of their works. In the case of YouTube, an artist needs to get hundreds of millions of views for their works to make any substantial amount of money.

171. This is known as the value gap, which may or may not be addressed by the copyright laws and requires new business models to ensure that the rights holders are properly compensated. Here the role of the intermediary service provider – Internet Service Providers ISPs) is crucial but limited based on the extent to which the ISP can be liable and including the safe harbour provisions. It is not their duty to monitor the works that are uploaded online.

172. The other issue relates to digitisation of works and lending by public libraries online. The issue of cross-border exchange arises especially due to the borderless nature of the Internet, once the works have been uploaded, they can be accessed by anyone who has access to the Internet. However, some technological protection measures have to be employed to limit access to only those who are authorised to access the works.

---

67. For further reading, *see* Simon Stokes (2014) *Digital Copyright Law and Practice* 4th Edition Oxford and Portland, Oregon pp. 177–179.

III. Liability of ISPs

173. ISPs or ISPs are entities that offer transmission, routing or provide connections for digital online communication to allow users to choose what to access at their own convenience. This is done without altering the content being transmitted. Examples include:

(a) Network operators including mobile and data service providers such as Safaricom and MTN.
(b) Network Infrastructure Providers such as CISCO, Liquid, Access Kenya.
(c) Internet Service/Access Providers such as Wananchi, Jamii Telecom and Access Kenya.
(d) Social Networks such as Facebook, Twitter and WhatsApp.
(e) Search Engines such as Google, Yahoo, Web crawler among others.

174. It is not possible for one to monitor use of their works online and there are millions of copyright works that are uploaded and downloaded online. We have discussed the right of making available, which is exclusively granted to the rights holder. However, third parties may make the work available without permission from the rights holder. There is no obligation to place the liability on the end user under the law making the ISPs targets as they are deemed to facilitate these Acts. This is based on the principle of secondary liability as the ISPs are deemed to be in control of what is uploaded on their networks. However, this liability is limited and the ISPs can rely on what is known as 'Safe Harbours'. In Africa, only Ghana and South Africa have made provisions for liability of ISPs and safe harbours and these are contained in the Electronic Transactions Act. ISPs under these laws shall be excluded from liability if:

(a) They are mere conduits as information is simply transmitted within the network or they provide access to a communication network including automatic, intermediate and transient storage of works. This is only limited to cases where the ISP does not initiate the transmission, select the receiver and does not in any way select or modify the information/content of the transmission.
(b) Caching, which is the automatic, intermediate and temporary storage of information solely for making a more efficient onward transmission, provided the ISP does not modify the information, complies with the conditions and rules for the transmission and does not interfere with legitimate technology employed to obtain the data. The ISP will not be liable if it acts expeditiously to comply with the takedown notice.
(c) Hosting which includes storage of information provided the ISP has no actual knowledge of the infringement and acts expeditiously once issued with a takedown notice.
(d) The ISP will not be liable for merely providing information location tools. For instance, referring users to links that contain infringing works by using information location tools such as a directory, index, reference, pointer or hyperlink

where it has no knowledge of the infringing activities. These provisions are very important especially in relation to user-generated content through platforms such as YouTube.

(e) If the ISP complies with the takedown notice expeditiously to ensure that the infringement is curtailed, they will not be held liable. It is important to note that this may take a while as there is a need to verify the authenticity of the take-down notice to avoid malicious or fake notices. In South Africa, the law requires proper investigation and takedown has to be through a court order. In Ghana, the law makes one liable for providing false information.

175. The proposed Electronic Transactions Bill in Kenya included the above provisions but it has yet to be submitted to parliament. The KECOBO has also included provisions on liability of ISPs and safe harbours in the Copyright (Amendment) Bill 2017.

Chapter 2. Patents

176. Until 1989, the Kenyan patent system was entirely dependent upon the British patent system. In order to obtain patent protection in Kenya, an applicant was required to apply for and obtain a patent certificate in the UK, which certificate would then be re-registered in Kenya with local effect. There existed no legal provision for re-examination of the UK certificate.

177. The Industrial Property Act (IPA) of 1989 divorced Kenya from the UK system and instituted the Kenya Industrial Patent Office (KIPO) with the mandate to examine and administer patent applications. By 1994, the patent office was granting patents from international and local applicants. Grants were slow at first – two in 1994, one in 1995 – but increased from 1996. In response to requirements under TRIPS, Kenya passed the IPA 2001, followed by the Industrial Property Regulations 2002. The IPA 2001 created the Kenya Industrial Property Institute (KIPI), which replaced KIPO and remains the current patent-granting authority in Kenya.

178. Today, KIPI is one of the most active national patent offices on the continent, and also one of the only national offices to carry out substantive examination of applications. A substantial majority of patent applications have foreign applicants, whereas nearly all utility model applications have local applicants.

§1. Sources – Legislation and International Treaties

179. The primary source of patent law in Kenya is the IPA 2001 and the associated regulations. Specifically, Parts III-XI of the IPA 2001 are devoted to patents. Parts XV-XVII provide general provisions about infringement and enforcement that apply to patents as well as other rights in the IPA 2001. The IPA 2001 has been amended three times, in 2002, 2007, and 2017. The IPA Regulations were passed and came into force in 2002.

180. In addition to the IPA 2001, a number of international instruments affect the patent law in Kenya. Chief among these is the Agreement on TRIPS. As a WTO member, Kenya was required to be TRIPS compliant according to the schedule that applied to developing countries. The IPA 2001 was passed in partial compliance of that requirement.

181. Kenya is also a member of the Paris Convention and the Patent Cooperation Treaty (PCT), and KIPI acts as a receiving office for PCT applications. Accordingly, the provisions of these treaties affect the framework for patent law in Kenya as described below.

182. Finally, Kenya is a member of the Harare Protocol within the African Regional Intellectual Property Organization (ARIPO). The Harare Protocol implements a patent system (somewhat similar to the European Patent Organization) within 19 English-speaking countries in Africa. Patents granted through ARIPO can designate Kenya, in which case the patent is treated as equivalent to a nationally-granted patent.

§2. Patentable Subject Matter

183. A Kenyan patent provides government-granted rights for an 'invention' – i.e., a solution to a specific problem in a field of technology. Any subject matter that satisfies this requirement can be patented, apart from the exclusions that are laid out below.

184. Inventions that are excluded from patentability are:

- discoveries, scientific theories and mathematical methods;
- schemes, rules or methods for doing business, performing purely mental acts or playing games;
- methods for treatment of the human or animal body by surgery or therapy, as well as diagnostic methods practised in relation thereto, except products for use in any such methods;
- mere presentation of information; and
- Public Health related methods of use or uses of any molecule or other substances whatsoever used for the prevention or treatment of any disease which the Minister responsible for matters relating to health may designate as a serious health hazard or as a life threatening disease.[68]

It is worth noting that the pre-2001 patent law included an identical list but for one additional item: computer programs. The removal of computer programs from the list of excluded subject matter in the IPA 2001 implies that such inventions are patentable. In fact, several granted patents are directed to software-implemented inventions, and some claims are even directed explicitly to software.[69]

185. Additionally, the following is non-patentable subject matter: plant varieties as provided for in the Seeds and Plant Varieties Act, but not parts thereof or products of biotechnological processes; and inventions contrary to public order, morality, public health and safety, principles of humanity and environmental conservation.[70]

68. Section 21(3) Industrial Property Act 2001.
69. Nzomo, V., and Rutenberg, I., 'Patenting the Un-Patentable? A review of patentable subject matter in granted patent claims: Kenya as a case study,' *South African Intellectual Property Law Journal*, (2017) v. 5, 58–74.
70. Section 26 Industrial Property Act 2001.

§3. Conditions of Patentability

186. Section 22 of the IPA 2001 states that an invention is suitable for a patent when it is new, involves an inventive step, and is industrially applicable or is a new use. Since patent offices examine applications rather than inventions, however, it is more appropriate to state that the invention is suitable for patent when that invention *as claimed* is new, involves an inventive step, and is industrially applicable or is a new use. The requirement that an invention is new is also referred to as the 'novelty' requirement. The requirement that an invention involves an inventive step may also be referred to as the 'non-obvious' requirement.

187. An invention is new when that invention as claimed is not anticipated by prior art. Neither the IPA 2001 nor the implementing Regulations define 'anticipated', so during substantive examination the patent office examiners have some degree of liberty to decide whether a particular piece of prior art is sufficiently close to the claimed invention to be anticipatory. Nevertheless, even minor differences between a claimed invention and a prior art reference are likely sufficient to pass the test for novelty.

188. An invention involves an inventive step when, compared to the most relevant prior art, the claimed invention would not have been obvious to a person skilled in the art to which the invention pertains as of the effective filing date of the application. Again, neither the IPA 2001 nor the Regulations define 'obvious', nor do they provide the standard for a 'person skilled in the art'. These terms are widely used in patent laws throughout the world, and a jurisdiction may use its own standard or may apply standards used in other jurisdictions.

189. An invention is industrially applicable if it can be used in any kind of industry. The IPA 2001 cites agriculture, medicine, and fishery as non-exhaustive examples of industries. Neither the IPA 2001 nor the Regulations provide any further guidance as to what constitutes a 'new use'.

§4. Formalities (Procedure for Grant and Obtaining Patent Protection)

190. Patent applications in Kenya are filed at the Kenya Industrial Property Institute, KIPI, in Nairobi. Consistent with the IPA of 2001 the application includes the following parts: a request; a description; one or more claims; one or more drawings (where necessary); and an abstract. A formalities examination is carried out shortly after the filing date, and if certain minimum criteria are satisfied, a filing date and serial number are assigned to the application. The applicant is also invited to correct any defects identified in the formalities examination.

191. The request that accompanies an application must indicate whether the application is for a provisional application or for a final application. Provisional applications are not examined and expire automatically twelve months after the filing date. A final application must therefore be filed within twelve months of the provisional application filing date in order to claim priority to the provisional application; recall that the priority application must be pending when the later application is filed in order for priority to be claimed.

192. Eighteen months after the filing date, the application is published by KIPI. There is now a provision to request early publication, and KIPI cannot grant the application until after the application has been published. Examination and grant of the application take the normal path as described above.

193. Substantive examination in the Kenyan patent office is based on a worldwide search for prior art. In some countries, including Kenya, the patent law allows a grace period during which time an applicant's own publications or activities are not considered prior art. The IPA 2001 allows for a grace period of one year after an inventor publishes details of an invention or uses the invention in public. During the grace period, the inventor's publication or use will not bar the filing of a patent application claiming the disclosed invention.

194. Regarding a post-grant opposition period, the IPA 2001 allows revocation hearings to be initiated in the Industrial Property Tribunal (IPT). Proceedings in the High Court may also result in revocation of a patent. For example, *in Duplex Engineers Ltd. v. Jaswinder Singh Sehmi* (1997), the High Court found that the patented invention was in the public domain because the defendant had installed it in his factory and used the invention for two years. Such use had been observed by numerous people and was therefore considered a public use. The public use was sufficient to render the invention unpatentable, and the court ordered revocation of the patent in question.

§5. Ownership and Transfer (Assignment: Licenses)

I. Assignment and Ownership

195. Like other forms of IPR, patents have many of the characteristics of real property. For example, they can be sold or licensed by the patent owner, serve as collateral for a loan, and be bequeathed upon the death of a patent owner. A critical factor in any transaction or legal action involving a patent is, then, determination of the owner of the patent.

196. In the absence of any other claims or assignments, the default owner of a patent is the inventor(s) of the invention described by the claims of the patent. The inventor is also the individual with the first right to be an applicant – i.e., to file a patent application towards the invention. Where more than one individual was involved in developing the claimed invention, co-inventors may be named and have the right to file a patent application as co-applicants.

197. A number of situations may shift ownership and cause the inventor to lose their right to be an applicant.[71] The most common situation where the applicant is not the inventor is that of an employee/employer relationship. Where the inventor is an employee, the employer becomes the default applicant and patent owner for all inventions resulting from the employee's activities under the employment contract. Similarly, where an invention results from a contract for service or a commissioned work, the person having commissioned the work becomes the patent applicant.

198. The above situations can be modified with an employment agreement or contract stating otherwise with respect to ownership of inventions. In all of these cases, and notwithstanding the identity of the patent applicant, the inventor is identified on any patent application as the inventor.

199. At any time after the filing of a patent application, the application or the patent(s) granted from the application may be assigned or licensed by the applicant to a third party.[72] In the case of a license, the licensor may decide to license all or a subset of the rights granted by the patent. Licenses may be exclusive or non-exclusive.[73]

II. Licensing

200. Part X of the IPA deals with contractual licenses, and largely (although not entirely) restates basic principles of licensing. For example, section 64 states that a licensee under a license contract is entitled to do any act reserved for the owner of a patent[74] unless provided otherwise by the license contract creating the license. Some notable provisions of the Act are discussed below. It should be noted that Section X applies to patents as well as utility model certificates (UMCs).

201. For example, under the Act, a license is not sub-licensable by default. That is, in the absence of any provision to the contrary in the license contract, the licensee may not grant any of the rights referred to in section 54 of the Act (the rights of the owner) to a third party.[75]

202. The Act states that all license contracts are to be in writing[76] and must be registered with KIPI.[77] Outside Kenya, some jurisdictions may allow implied licenses through the conduct of the parties. For example, in the United States case

71. Section 32, Industrial Property Act 2001.
72. Section 62, Industrial Property Act 2001.
73. Although the issue has not yet been settled in Kenya, in some jurisdictions licenses are generally acceptable only provided that the license expires Continuing royalties even after the patent has expired is frowned upon as an improper means for indefinitely extending patent term. In other jurisdictions courts allow such provisions on the basis of freedom-of-contract principles.
74. Refer to s. 54, *Industrial Property Act*, Cap. 509 Laws of Kenya.
75. Section 64(2), *Industrial Property Act*, Cap. 509 Laws of Kenya.
76. Section 67, *Industrial Property Act*, Cap. 509 Laws of Kenya.
77. *Ibid.*, ss 68,70.

of *Integrated Global Concepts, Inc. v. J2 Global, Inc.*[78] the court held that a patent license may be implied from the conduct of the parties by relying on the equitable doctrine of estoppel. Citing a prior case from the United States Federal Circuit, the court stated, '*An implied license by equitable estoppel requires that: "(1) the patentee, through statements or conduct, gave an affirmative grant of consent or permission to make, use, or sell to the alleged infringer; (2) the alleged infringer relied on that statement or conduct; and (3) the alleged infringer would, therefore, be materially prejudiced if the patentee is allowed to proceed with its claim ...* "'[79] The existence of an implied license can potentially be used as a defence for patent infringement.

203. The freedom of the licensor to grant any of his rights through licensing also implies the right of the licensor to deny the licensee certain rights and/or place restrictions on the rights granted. The IPA 2001 tries to protect licensees from potentially unreasonable licensors by allowing the Managing Director of KIPI to refuse to register a license contract if s/he is of the opinion that the contract imposes unjustified restrictions on the licensee with the consequence that the contract taken as whole would be detrimental to Kenya's economic interests.[80]

204. The IPA provides for compulsory licenses in certain situations, particularly by introducing a 'working' requirement. That is, a compulsory license may be obtained at any time after four years from the filing date of an application or three years from the grant of a patent (whichever period expires last), by applying to the IPT on the grounds that the market for the patented invention in Kenya is not being supplied on reasonable terms. This license, however, shall not be granted if the owner of the patent can satisfy the Tribunal that circumstances exist which justify the fact that the market for the patented invention is not being supplied at all or at reasonable terms.[81]

205. The Tribunal will only grant a compulsory license if the person applying for the license:

(1) Satisfies the Tribunal that he has asked the owner of the patent for a contractual license but has failed to obtain the license on reasonable commercial terms and within a reasonable time; and
(2) offers guarantees satisfactory to the Tribunal to work the invention in question, remedy any of its deficiencies or to satisfy the requirements which gave rise to the request.[82]

---

78. Case No. 5:12-cv-03434-RMW (PSG) (N.D. Cal. Mar. 20, 2014).
79. *Ibid., citing Winbond Electronics Corp. v. Int'l Trade Comm'n, 262 F.3d 1363, 1374 opinion corrected, 275 F.3d 1344 (Fed. Cir. 2001).*
80. *Ibid.*, s. 69.
81. *Ibid.*, s. 72.
82. *Ibid.*, s. 74(1).

206. If the Tribunal grants a compulsory license, then it will proceed to fix the terms of the license, ensuring that the license: is limited in scope and duration; is limited predominantly for the supply of the local market; doesn't entitle the licensee to grant further licenses; is non-exclusive; and provides for the remuneration of the owner of the patent which is equitable with due regard to the circumstances of the case.[83]

207. Section 76 allows for the transfer of compulsory licenses only with respect to the industrial undertaking in which the invention is used, and only with the consent of the Tribunal. The Tribunal will not, for example, grant such a transfer to a different entity for a different purpose than the original application that gave rise to the original compulsory license.

208. The Tribunal also has the power to cancel or modify a compulsory license, as per sections 77 of the Act. The cancellation process is instituted, for example by an application to the Tribunal by any interested party. The application must show that either the licensee has failed to comply with the terms of the license or that the conditions which justified the grant of the license have ceased to exist and are unlikely to recur provided that the legitimate interests of the license are adequately protected.

209. Any grant, cancellation or variation of compulsory licenses must be registered. The registration is done when the Tribunal instructs the Managing Director of KIPI to record the grant, cancellation or variation in the register without the payment of any fee.[84]

§6. Scope of Exclusive Rights

210. A patent grants to the patentee specific rights with respect to the invention. For patents pertaining to a product, those rights including the right to exclude others from making, importing, offering for sale, selling, stocking for the purpose of offering for sale, and using the product. Patent rights are exclusionary rather than permissive. Accordingly, a patent does not grant the right to sell or use the patented invention, and where a patented invention violates or fails to comply with other non-patent statutes and regulations, the patent owner does not have the right to sell or use the invention. Furthermore, where a patented invention involves technology that is patented by a third party, the patent owner is not entitled to sell the invention without the permission of the third party.

---

83. *Ibid.*, s. 75.
84. *Ibid.*, s. 78.

§7. Limitations and Exceptions to the Scope of Patent Protection: Compulsory Licenses

211. The Intellectual Property Act 2001 contains a variety of provisions for the government to apply a compulsory license to a granted patent. Principle among those provisions, which is commonly referred to as a 'working' requirement in other jurisdictions, states that a compulsory license may be granted for any patented invention on the grounds that a market or the patented invention is not being supplied on reasonable terms in Kenya. Such compulsory licenses are only available three years after the grant of the patent or four years from the filing date of the application.

212. A compulsory license may also be granted for the Government of Kenya (or an authorised representative of the Government) to exploit a patented invention where the public interest so requires. Public interest includes reasons of health, nutrition, national security, and environmental conservation. Compulsory licenses of this nature are, throughout the world, relatively rare. India's decades-old Patents Act has had a similar provision, but the first compulsory license was not granted in India until 2012. Nevertheless such provisions are controversial and have been the subject of much debate and literature attention.

§8. Duration of Protection: Maintaining and Terminating Patent Protection

213. As with other countries that are TRIPS compliant, the term of a patent granted in Kenya under the IPA 2001 expires after twenty years from the filing date of the patent application.[85] Annual fees are required in order to maintain a pending patent application as well as a granted patent.[86]

§9. Infringement and Remedies

214. Infringement occurs when a party, without authorisation from a patent owner, does the following: makes, imports, offers for sale, sells, uses, or stocks for the purpose of selling or using a patented product; makes, imports, offers for sale, sells, uses, or stocks for the purpose of selling or using a product obtained using a patent process; or uses a patent process.

215. A patentee may obtain relief for acts of infringement in the form of an injunction to restrain the infringement and/or damages from any person carrying out

85. *See* s. 60 of the Industrial Property Act 2001. The IPA2001 does not explicitly state that priority claims should be considered when calculating the patent term, although in other patent laws in other jurisdictions priority claims other than, perhaps, provisional applications are always considered when determining the filing date.
86. Section 61, Industrial Property Act 2001.

the infringement. Furthermore, once a patent has been granted, unauthorised acts carried out prior to the grant of the patent but after the publication of the patent application may be considered infringing and actionable, provided that the infringing party had actual notice of the patent application publication and the potential infringement. Certain exceptions apply to infringing activities, such as bona fide prior use (i.e., use that occurs prior to the filing of a patent application), use for scientific research, and use under a compulsory license imposed by the government.

216. An independent IPT is authorised under the IPA 2001 and serves two main functions. The first function is to hear appeals by patent applicants against decisions taken by the patent office. For example, decisions by the patent office to reject a patent application or to grant a compulsory license may be appealed to the IPT.

217. The second function is to act as a Court of First Instance for infringement proceedings between a patent owner and an accused infringing party. The IPT has authority to grant any relief provided under the IPA 2001, and IPT decisions may be appealed to the High Court of Kenya. Similarly, the IPT may also hear requests for a declaration of non-infringement. Such requests are typically made by individuals concerned that they may be sued by a patent owner for infringement.

218. In addition to the IPT, the High Court of Kenya shares original jurisdiction to hear patent infringement actions. Such jurisdiction is provided not by the IPA 2001, but by the High Court's Constitutionally granted unlimited original jurisdiction in criminal and civil matters. '[T]he fact that an Act of Parliament provides for a forum for determining dispute does not of itself divest the High Court of its original jurisdiction to try all civil matters' (*Apex Creative Ltd v. Karatasi Industries Ltd*, 2011). Numerous cases have, however, observed that the IPT might be the most suitable forum for patent infringement cases due to the technical competency of the Tribunal panelists (*Ukwala Supermarkets Ltd. v. Paul Mburu Wainaina* 2006; *Sanitam Services v. Kentainer* 1999; *David Engineering Ltd. v. Steel Structures* 2007).

I. Case Law

A. Sanitam Services (EA) Ltd v. Rentokil Initial (K) Ltd and Kentainers (K) Ltd

219. This is a series of cases in the High Court, Appeals Court, and Intellectual Property Tribunal of Kenya involving Sanitam Services (EA) Ltd as plaintiff and patent holder. At issue were infringement and validity of ARIPO Patent No. AP773, which patent describes a 'foot operated Sanitary/disposal bin comprising a container (1) closable by a cover (2), with a disposal lid 3) at the top, with the disposal lid being displaceable, by a foot operated pedal (4) and a lift lever (5), to move between open and closed positions. The bin is defined such that the user cannot see the contents of the container (I), waste scavengers cannot have access to the contents, emissions of unpleasant odour is reduced and the contents cannot spill out if the bin is overturned.' Due to the timing of the alleged infringement, the courts applied the IPA of 1989 (Cap. 509) rather than the updated IPA of 2001.

220. In the original case in the High Court of Kenya,[87] the plaintiff Sanitam Services alleged that the defendants were selling a foot operated bins that infringed the ARIPO granted patent. The plaintiff's case failed because, according to the judge, Sanitam failed to prove that it had timely obtained a patent over its foot operated sanitary bin. In particular, according to the judge, the plaintiff had been producing the product for two years before they applied for the patent, and on that evidence the judge stated 'I would be tempted to think that the plaintiff possibly sought for and obtained patent to stop clear competition that was already in the market ... ' Furthermore the judge remarked that there was no evidence of infringement: 'I was not shown any bin exactly similar to the Plaintiff which was allegedly manufactured wholly or imported in part by the Defendants ... ' For these reasons the court found that the defendants had not infringed Sanitam's rights, and dismissed the case.

221. Sanitam Services appealed the High Court's decision, and in the appeal[88] claimed that it designed and invented a foot-operated litter/sanitary disposal bin in 1997 for use in the hygienic storage and disposal of sanitary towels, tampons, surgical dressings, serviettes and other waste material. The appellant claimed that it had submitted an application for registration to the Kenya Industrial Property Office (KIPO, the predecessor to the current KIPI) but by the time the suit was determined KIPO had not processed the application for issuance of the patent. The appellant further claimed that, notwithstanding the situation in the Kenyan national patent office, they had applied for and obtained patent protection in Kenya in the form of ARIPO patent No. AP773. The respondents continued to argue that the foot operated bin had been in the market for many years before Sanitam Services registered for the ARIPO and KIPO patents, and that the invention was therefore not patentable. The judge granted an injunction against the defendants with effect from 16 December 1999 – i.e., from the date that the appellant brought to the attention of the court and the defendants the existence of the granted ARIPO patent. However the Court of Appeal did not award Sanitam any damages on the grounds that Sanitam had not discharged the onus of proof.

222. In a parallel action, Sanitam Services also brought proceedings in Kenya's Intellectual Property Tribunal (IPT) against Rentokil and Kentainers.[89] In that case, the IPT concluded by revoking ARIPO patent number AP773. On appeal,[90] Sanitam applied for and received a stay of the revocation order of the IPT pending a hearing.[91] As of the writing of this book, there remains no further judicial activity on the matter.

87. *Sanitam Services Ltd. v. Rentokil Initial (K) Ltd.* and another, Civ. Case 58 of 1999.
88. *Sanitam Services Ltd. v. Rentokil Initial (K) Ltd.* and another, Civil Appeal 228 of 2004 [2006] eKLR.
89. *Sanitam Services Ltd. v. Rentokil Initial (K) Ltd.* and another, Nairobi Intellectual Property Tribunal No. 5 of 1999.
90. *Sanitam Services Ltd. v. Kentainers*, Civil Appeal 23 of 2014.
91. The application by Sanitam Services was based on notice of motion Order 42, rule 6 of the Civil Procedure Rules.

223. In another case brought by Sanitam Services before the High Court of Kenya, ARIPO patent AP 773 was once again at issue.[92,93] The plaintiff, Sanitam Services (EA) Ltd, filed suit against the defendant, Bins Nairobi Services Ltd, seeking orders of a permanent injunction and an interlocutory injunction to restrain the defendant from infringing its patent in respect of foot operated sanitary bins.

224. The defendant responded with two defences: non-infringement, as well as invalidity of the asserted patent. Specifically, the defendant claimed that the same or similar bins had been used the world over prior to the registration of the patent, such that the patent was anticipated by the prior art – i.e., the patent was invalid and should never have been granted. The defendant also stated that their foot-operated bin was not similar to that of the plaintiff, such that there was no infringement, regardless of the validity of the patent. The court examined these claims and found in favour of the plaintiff.

225. Regarding the validity of the patent, the court gave deference to the decision of ARIPO to grant the patent (and KIPI's decision not to oppose ARIPO's grant). The court noted that the defendant should initiate invalidation or revocation proceedings under section 103 of the IPA, 2001 if the defendant wishes to challenge the validity of the patent as a defence to infringement.

226. Regarding non-infringement, the court did not conduct a thorough analysis of whether the defendant's bins infringed the granted patent, but rather stated that the plaintiff had established a prima facie case with a likelihood of success sufficient to warrant at least a temporary injunction.

227. In summary, therefore, the court held in a preliminary fashion in favour of the plaintiff, thus granting an interlocutory injunction pending determination of the issue of infringement. The court cited, in support of this decision, the success of the same plaintiff in the Court of Appeal in 2004.[94]

228. In addition to the above cases, numerous other lawsuits have been brought by and against Sanitam Services pertaining to AP 773.[95]

---

92. *Sanitam Services Ltd. v. Bins (Nairobi) Services Ltd.*, HCCC Civil Suit 597 of 2007.
93. *Sanitam Services Ltd. v. Bins (Nairobi) Services Ltd.* [2008] eKLR.
94. *Sanitam Services Ltd. v. Rentokil Initial (K) Ltd.* and another, Civil Appeal 228 of 2004 [2006] eKLR.
95. *Sanitam Services (EA) Ltd. v. Tamia Ltd.* & 16 Others [2012] eKLR; *Sanitam Services (EA) Ltd. v. Kenya Pipeline Civil* Case No. 471 of 2013; *Republic v. Public Procurement Administrative Review Board & 2 others Ex Parte – Sanitam Services (E.A) Ltd.* MISC. APPL. No. 204 OF 2013 [2013] eKLR; *Chemserve Cleaning Services Ltd. v. Sanitam Services Ltd.* No. 57 of 2008.

B. Pfizer Inc. v. Cosmos Ltd, IP Tribunal Case No. 49 of 2006

229. The plaintiff claimed that by producing the drug 'Zi Throx,' the defendant had infringed its patent protecting azithromycin dehydrate and a method of manufacture thereof. The patent was an ARIPO-granted patent validated in Kenya.[96] The defendant argued that the patent on the product had expired in US where it was also registered and that there were many products imported from other countries that contained the same product. The Tribunal stated that the fact that the patent had expired in US does not affect the patent in Kenya as patents are territorial. The defendant also argued that they were allowed to infringe the patent in line with the 'peace clause' in the TRIPS agreement, as the drug was used to fight opportunistic diseases associated with HIV/AIDS. The tribunal refuted this claim on the grounds that the drug was not a front line drug fighting HIV/AIDS, and that the defendant did not have a voluntary license or compulsory license. The Tribunal therefore concluded that the defendant did infringe the patent. The Tribunal granted the plaintiff an injunction stopping the defendant from continuing to use the protected product and allowed the plaintiff to make an election to the preferred remedy.

§10. Overlapping and Relation to Other IP Laws

230. Compared with copyright and trademarks, patents are significantly more difficult to obtain. The substantive examination process is designed to exclude from patentability any inventions that were previously known and documented anywhere in the world. Substantive examination is also designed to reject any applications that are insufficiently detailed such that they cannot perform the public disclosure element of patenting.

231. Both patents and copyright prohibit unauthorised copying of the thing protected, but the exclusionary powers granted by a patent are, in many ways, significantly more effective. Copyright does not prohibit independent creation of a copyrighted work (e.g., independent development of a software that carries out the same function of a previously copyrighted software) and does not prohibit the existence of identical works (e.g., two photographs taken independently but of the same scene or object). Patents provide protection against both of these scenarios, at least to some degree.

232. Patents are exclusively provided for items or processes that are 'useful'; have some industrial utility. In comparison, copyright vests in works that are original or creative, but are not necessarily useful. Often, patents and copyright are granted to different aspects of a single product (for instance, a patented device and the copyrighted user manual and advertising brochure for the device), but occasionally, and particularly in the case of software, patents and copyright can exist for the same product.

96. ARIPO Patent No. 44.

233. Unlike trademarks, which can typically be renewed indefinitely provided that the trademark remains in use, patents are always time limited. Statutes determine the effective term of a patent. Patent term may be reduced for instance by failure of the patentee to pay appropriate fees and/or may be extended for example by extension to account for delays in obtaining necessary government regulatory approvals for the patented product. Upon expiry of a patent, the invention described in the patent can be used by anyone without the need for permission by the patentee, provided that there are no other unexpired patents or other IPR covering some element of the invention.

Chapter 3. Utility Models

§1. Sources – Legislation

234. Part XII of the IPA 2001 provides for UMCs in Kenya. An applicant can file directly for utility model protection. Alternatively, a patent application can be converted to a utility model application, and vice versa, upon filing the appropriate form with KIPI.

235. Furthermore, it is possible to obtain a UMC through ARIPO, designating Kenya.

§2. The Protection of Utility Models

236. The Utility Model carries exclusionary rights that are equivalent to patents, but for a shorter period of time – Utility Models have a term of ten years measured from the grant date as opposed to twenty years measured from the filing date for patents. The reduced term of protection is offset by a reduced standard of patentability. In order to obtain a UMC, the claims must only describe an innovation that is industrially useful and novel – the inventive step that is required for patent protection is not necessary for a UMC.

237. In 2014, citing a lack of authority under the IPA 2001, KIPI ceased substantive examination of UMC applications. Accordingly, all utility model applications that pass formalities examination are automatically granted as UMCs. A registration system rather than an examination system for utility models is typical among countries that offer such protection.

238. Although most African countries offer protection via UMC, such protection is not universal and is absent in some developed countries. Regimes similar to UMCs may be known by a variety of names in other jurisdictions, such as 'functional designs' in South Africa. Under certain circumstances, international filing systems such as the PCT and ARIPO are available to utility model applicants.

Chapter 4. Trademarks

239. Trademarks are one of the forms of IPR that are recognised and protected by law in Kenya. Kenya's legislative history on trademarks can be traced to Act No. 51 of 1955. This statute was enacted to primarily protect the interests and businesses of the British citizens living in the country. Being a British colony, the Kenya trademark law was modelled on the 1938 English Trade Marks Act. The 1955 Act established a Trade Mark Register whose entries were limited. Protection was extended to trademarks after prior examination. It allowed registration of trademarks for goods only. Through various amendments the Act has allowed the registration of service marks.

§1. Sources – Legislation and International Treaties

I. Domestic Law

240. The reigning legislation in trademarks in Kenya is the Trade Marks Act (Cap. 509) Laws of Kenya together with the regulations made thereunder. While the Act is based on successive amendments to the 1955 Act, the last major overhaul was undertaken in 2007. Prior, in 2002, the statute had been amended to allow the adoption of the Nice International Classification of Goods and Services for the description of the goods and services prior to registration among other amendments. A proposal to completely overhaul the entire statute was mooted via a Trade Marks Bill, 2015. However, the draft Bill is yet to be formally presented to the National Assembly for debate.

241. The Anti-Counterfeit Act, 2008 is also a relevant statute in complementing the Trade Marks Act (Cap. 506) in enforcement matters. This statute establishes the Anti-Counterfeit Authority, a state agency with powers to prosecute infringers of IPR including trademarks. The Anti-Counterfeit Act, 2008 also establishes a recordal system requiring trademarks related to goods imported into Kenya irrespective of the place of their registration to be recorded with the Anti-Counterfeit Authority.[97] This system of recordation came into force on 18 January 2019. However, regulations to prescribe the process of recordation are yet to be enacted.

242. Besides the aforementioned statutes, there are a number of international treaties and conventions that are relevant. At the same time, there are a number of international conventions to which Kenya has ratified that are applicable particularly with respect to trademarks registration process.

97. Anti-Counterfeit Act (2008), s. 34B.

II. International Law

243. The relevant international instruments applicable in Kenya include the below.

A. *The Paris Convention on Protection of Industrial Property*

244. The Paris Convention applies to all forms of IP including trademarks and service marks. There are two main principles that are provided for under this Convention that cut across the enumerated IPR including trademarks and service marks: national treatment and the right of priority. The national treatment principle requires each Contracting Party to grant the same protection to nationals of other Contracting States that it grants its own nationals. The national treatment principle is also extended to nationals on non-Contracting Parties if they are domiciled or have a real and effective industrial or commercial establishment in a Contracting State.[98] The right of priority on the other hand means that on the basis of a regular first application in one of the Contracting States, the applicant may, within a certain period of time (six months for trademarks) apply for protection in any of the other Contracting States. These subsequent applications will be regarded as if they have been filed on the same day as the first application.[99] Other common rules provided for under the Paris Convention concern State right to refuse registration and prohibition of use of marks that consist without authorisations, state emblems, armorial bearings and flags of other Convention States and international organisations such as the Red Cross.[100]

245. Protection of well-known marks is also provided for in the Paris Convention. Under the Convention, each Contracting State must refuse registration and prohibit the use of marks that constitute a reproduction, imitation or translation, liable to create confusion, of a mark used for identical and similar goods and considered by the competent authority of that State to be *well known in that State* and to already belong to a person entitled to the benefits of the Convention.[101] Section 15A of the Trade Marks Act (cap. 506) makes provision for protection of well-known marks, and was recently the subject of litigation in the High Court in *Sony Corporation v. Sony Holdings Limited.*[102] In this case, Sony Corporation, opposed the application for registration of the trademark, 'SONY' by Sony Holdings on the ground that in the classes where there were overlaps, it was the exclusive owner of the 'SONY' brand in Kenya, and in the other classes, is a well-known mark in Kenya. The court in its finding stated that among others, the Registrar of Trademarks should have been asked to take judicial notice of the notoriety of the mark so that then he could invoke the doctrine of well-known marks.

98. https://www.wipo.int/treaties/en/ip/paris/summary_paris.html.
99. https://www.wipo.int/treaties/en/ip/paris/summary_paris.html.
100. The prohibitions have been replicated in Rules 15, 16 and 17 of the Trade Marks Rules.
101. https://www.wipo.int/treaties/en/ip/paris/summary_paris.html.
102. [2018] eKLR.

246. Kenya acceded to the Paris Convention in 1965 and, most of its provisions have been adopted and provided for under the Trade Marks Act.

B. The Madrid Agreement and the Madrid and Protocol

247. The Madrid Agreement establishes the Madrid System of International Registration of Marks.[103,104] This system enables protection of a mark in a large number of countries by obtaining an international registration that has effect in each of the designated countries that are a party to the system. As this system enables a single application for registration of a trademark to be launched in multiple jurisdictions at the same time, the system offers several advantages for trademark owners. One of the advantages is that the applicant only pays a single fee to the International Bureau. Secondly, the application is only launched in one language (English, French or Spanish). Similar advantages apply in maintaining and renewing a registration.

248. The Madrid Agreement and Protocol are parallel and independent, yet States may adhere to either or both of them.[105] Kenya acceded to the Madrid Agreement and Madrid Protocol in 1998 and accepts applications filed under the system.[106]

C. The 1957 Nice Agreement Concerning the International Classification of Goods and Services for the Purposes of the Registration of Marks

249. The main objective of the Nice Agreement is to establish a classification system of goods and services for the purposes of registering trademarks and service marks. As a result, the Agreement establishes a Special Union of Member States, which Union prepares, and revises the Nice Classification of Goods and Services for purposes of registration of trademarks. While Kenya is not a Member of the Union it has via the Trade Marks Act (Cap. 506) adopted the Nice Classification and its various revisions for administration and registration of trademarks.[107]

---

103. The 1891 Madrid Agreement Concerning the International Registration of Marks (Madrid Agreement) and the 1989 Madrid Protocol Relating to the Madrid Agreement Concerning the International Registration of Marks (Madrid Protocol).
104. *See* http://www.wipo.int/madrid/en/romarin/.
105. http://www.wipo.int/treaties/en/registration/madrid/summary_madrid_marks.html.
106. The Trade Marks (International Registration) Rules, 2003.
107. Section 6 of the Trade Marks Act provides that all marks registered for goods and services as described by the Nice Classification of Goods and Services or the Vienna Agreement for Figurative Elements of Marks. The Nice Classification has been severally amended with the current applicable edition being the Eleventh Edition.

D. The Banjul Protocol of on Marks

250. This Protocol is governed by the ARIPO. It is akin to the Madrid Agreement and Protocol but within the African context. It allows persons from the Protocol Member States to file a single application which can be effective in all the other Member Countries at the option of the applicant, upon designation.

251. Kenya has not ratified the Banjul Protocol. However, the Protocol is recognised under the Trade Marks Act. Section 40D of the Trade Marks Act provides that a trademark in respect of which Kenya is a designated state, registered by ARIPO by virtue of the Banjul Protocol, shall have the same effect and enjoy the same protection in Kenya as a trademark registered under the Act, unless the Registrar communicates to ARIPO, in respect of the application, a decision in accordance with the provisions of the Protocol, that the mark shall have no effect in Kenya. It is expected that the Protocol application procedures will be operationalised once this Protocol is ratified.

E. Vienna Agreement Establishing an International Classification of the Figurative Elements of Marks

252. The Vienna Agreement establishes a classification system for marks that consist of, or contain, figurative marks. The purpose of the classification is to facilitate trademark anticipation searches and obviate substantial classification work when documents are exchanged at the international level.[108]

253. Inasmuch as Kenya is not a party to the Vienna Agreement, the classification system established under this Agreement is domesticated under the Trade Marks Act (Cap. 506). Therefore Kenya relies on the Vienna classification system with respect to marks that consist of, or contain figurative elements, and does not need to draw up its own classification system.

§2. SUBJECT MATTER OF PROTECTION

254. The definition of a trademark in Kenya takes the form of differentiating whether the mark is proposed to be used in relation to goods or services. Under section 2 of the Trade Marks Act (Cap. 506) Laws of Kenya, a trademark means a mark used or proposed to be used:

(a) in relation to goods for the purpose of indicating a connection in the course of trade between the goods and some person having the right either as proprietor or as licensee to use the mark, whether with or without any indication of the identity of that person or distinguishing goods in relation to

108. https://www.wipo.int/treaties/en/classification/vienna/summary_vienna.html.

which the mark is used or proposed to be used from the same kind of goods connected in the course of trade with any person;

(b) in relation to services for the purpose of indicating that a particular person is connected, in the course of business, with the provision of those services, whether with or without any indication of the identity of that person or distinguishing services in relation to which the mark is used or proposed to be used from the same kind of services connected in the course of business with any other person.

255. The above definition does not extend or apply to certification trademarks. Certification trademarks are defined separately in section 40 of the same Act as marks adapted in relation to any goods to distinguish in the course of trade goods certified by any person in respect of origin, material, mode of manufacture, quality, accuracy or other characteristics from goods not so certified.

256. A general principle flowing from the above definition is that for marks to be considered trademarks under the law, they have to be used in the course of trade. Although trade in ordinary terms denotes profit making or dealings with an intention of positive gain, trade under trademarks law extends to all dealings including charity. To this extent, in section 2 of the Trade Marks Act trade is defined as any type of profession or business occupation in which a mark may be used within the meaning of the Act.[109] Therefore, a trademark can be used or applied on any good or service if such use is intended to serve one or all of the many functions of trademarks.

257. A trademark can take many forms and formats. Under Kenya law, a 'mark' may include a distinguishing guise, slogan, device, brand, heading, label, ticket, name, signature, word, letter or numeral or any combination thereof whether rendered in two-dimensional or three-dimensional form.[110] However, advances in brand innovation have led in some jurisdictions such as Europe and the United States for trademark forms to extend to sounds,[111] scents and smells,[112] tastes,[113] colours and holograms. Presently, however, Kenya only accepts trademarks that are in the form expressed in section 2 of the Trade Marks Act.

---

109. Trade Marks Act, s. 2.

110. *Ibid.*

111. For example US Trademark No.73553567 a sound trademark a Roaring Lion, is owned by Metro-Goldwyn-Mayer Studios, Inc. (MGM), an American media company, involved primarily in the production and distribution of feature films and television programs. Also *see* Regulation (EU) 2017/1001 Of the European Parliament and of the Council of 14 Jun. 2017 on the EU trade mark, Art. 4.

112. Although some of the challenges faced in this context includes establishing mechanisms to graphically represent smells in a satisfactory way.

113. As with olfactory marks, description challenges exist with respect to taste marks.

I. Types of Trademarks

258. There are five types of trademarks that are registrable in Kenya. They are:

Word Marks. These are trademarks that are coined from the letters that form the alphabet. They need not be decipherable or understandable to every person. For instance, they can be a combination of vowels only or simple letters.
Slogans. These are combination of two or more words to form a phrase. They are ordinarily short phrases as long phrases are more likely to confuse consumers.
Figurative Marks. They are also called device marks. These are the logos or pictorial representations of a mark.
Composite Marks. These are marks that comprise of two or more different elements that cannot be registered separately but when combined they become registrable.
3D marks. These are marks presented in a three-dimensional format. They are ordinarily the actual shape of a product or a product packaging.

II. Different Categories of Marks

259. The above trademarks may also be categorised into either of the following:

Ordinary trademarks. These are marks that are applied by traders for the sole purpose of distinguishing their goods or services in the market.
Certification marks. These are marks that are adapted in relation to any goods to distinguish in the course of trade goods certified by any person in respect of origin, material, mode of manufacture, quality, accuracy or other characteristics.[114]
Collective Marks. These are marks that belong to groups or association of people with common goal or interests. The mark therefore distinguishes the goods or services of the members of the association from those who are not members.[115]
Well-known Marks. These are marks that are usually protected, irrespective of whether they are registered or not, in respect of goods and services which are identical with, or similar to, those for which they have gained their reputation.[116] Section 15A of the Trade Marks Act (Cap. 506) provides for their protection under Kenya law.
Defensive Marks. These are an exemption to the ordinary marks as they are registered without the intention of using them. They are marks that are registered by proprietors who already own other well-known trademarks to bar third parties from using them. The sole purpose of these marks is to protect

114. Trade Marks Act, s. 40.
115. *Ibid.*, s. 40A.
116. https://www.wipo.int/sme/en/ip_business/marks/well_known_marks.htm.

the reputation of the well-known marks by preventing third parties from appropriating them on unrelated goods or services to those of the proprietors of the well-known marks. The registration of defensive marks allows the proprietors to prevent the use of the marks by third parties without necessarily instituting passing off actions.[117]

§3. CONDITIONS OF PROTECTION

260. For a mark or a sign to qualify to be a trademark within the meaning of the Trade Marks Act (Cap. 506) Laws of Kenya, it must possess the following characteristics.

I. It Must Indicate Connection Between the Goods or Services and the Person Having the Right to Use the Mark

261. The most fundamental function of a trademark is to indicate the connection between the goods or services it is applied against and the person having the right to use the mark. This person need not be the owner or the manufacturer of the goods. The person could be a licensee or an assignee or any other person authorised by law to use the mark. When properly applied, a trademark connects the goods or services with their origin. They are used to identify the source of goods or services by associating the goods with a particular trader. It creates a trade connection or relationship between the mark and the trademark owner. This function forms the basis of the actions of infringement and passing off.

II. It Must Be Used or Proposed to Be Used Against Some Goods and/or Services in the Course of Trade

262. A trademark has several functions including indicating connection between the proprietor and the goods. These functions can only be achieved when the trademark is in use. The use should also be in the course of trade. Inevitably this use has to be in the public domain and not private. In instances of a registered trademark, failure to use it constitutes a ground for removal or cancellation from the register.[118] In *Ansul BV v. Ajax Brandbeveiliging BV (2003)*[119] the ECJ held that genuine use of a mark entails use of the mark on the market for the goods or services protected by

117. Trade Marks Act, s. 30.
118. Section 29 of the Trade Marks Act allows for the removal of registered trademarks from the register in cases where it becomes apparent that they were registered with no bona fide intention of using them or where a period of five years from the date of the registration lapse before they are used.
119. Case C-40/01 R.P.C. 40, E.C.J. 11 Mar. 2003. Also reported in Cornish W., *Cases and Materials on Intellectual Property* 5th Edition, Sweet & Maxwell (2006) at p. 577.

that mark and not just internal use of the mark by the undertaking concerned. Therefore the use of the mark must be actual, against some goods or services and in the public domain.

III. It Must Be Capable of Being Represented Graphically

263. Like many other branches of IP law, trademark law does not protect ideas. To receive protection, the idea must be reduced or expressed in a particular manner. In the case of a trademark, the mark has to be capable of being graphically represented. It has to be conceived through or by at least one or more of the five human senses, but it cannot exist in abstract. Graphic representation enables the consumers to identify the mark when applied against some goods or services. It also facilitates the examination process when a proprietor applies for protection. It shows what the trademark is.

264. The mode of graphic representation of a trademark varies depending on the type of trademark in question. Some trademarks have to be described in more than one way for them to be considered to be graphically represented. For instance if the mark is a word, it has to be reduced into writing and may be represented in some artistic form, while for a logo the same must be drawn. For a sound mark,[120] the graphic representation is in the form of musical notations and a description of the sound. In *Libertel Groep v. Benelux-Merkenbureau (2004)* the Court held that presentation of a sample of a colour is not sufficient graphical description of a colour trademark because it might change with time but the trademark protection would not.[121]

IV. It Must Be Capable of Distinguishing those Goods or Services from Others

265. The essential function of a trademark is to distinguish goods or services of one enterprise from those of another. The Trade Marks Act (Cap. 506) Laws of Kenya defines a trademark to include a 'distinguishing guise' or a sign that distinguishes the goods or services of one trader to another.[122] Therefore, a trademark must be capable of distinguishing the goods or services of one enterprise from another in the market. A trademark must be distinctively different enough to be able to perform this function. The distinctiveness has to be in relation to the goods or services that the trademark is applied against. Examples of distinctive marks include

120. Besides the Roaring Lion mark, other sound marks include Nokia tune trademark (EUTM No. 071265356) and Samsung tune (USPTO No. 86521492). Also *see* EUTM No. 005090055 by Edgar Rice Burroughs, Inc.

121. E.C.R. I-3793, ECJ also reported in Cornish W. *Cases and Materials on Intellectual Property* 5th Edition, Sweet & Maxwell (2006) p. 559.

122. Trade Marks Act, s. 2.

Apple and *Samsung* for electronics; *Safaricom*, *Airtel* and *Orange* for telecommunication; *Weetabix*[123] for breakfast cereals among others. While some of these words (*Apple; Orange*) are ordinary English words, they have been applied against unconventional goods and services making them distinctive for the purposes of specific goods or services.

266. Distinctiveness of a mark can either be inherent in a mark or it can be acquired through use. This helps in determining whether or not a mark is capable of distinguishing the goods or services. Section 13(2) of the Trade Marks Act allows the Registrar of Trade Marks or the Court as the case may be to consider both inherent and acquired distinctiveness. A trademark can acquire distinctiveness through continuous use in reference to a particular good or service such that it identifies that good or service from the others; or shows connection between the certain goods or services to their proprietor of the goods or services in question.[124]

267. It is worth pointing out that a trademark may also lose its capacity to distinguish through continued use. In this case, such a trademark becomes generic of the goods or services it has been used against. For instance, *Thermos* was a trademark registered in the name of Thermos GmbH for vacuum flasks which became generic for the goods in which it was registered for.[125] *Sellotape* is a trademark owned by Henkel AG & Company KGaA that has now become generic for transparent, cellulose-based adhesive tapes.[126] These trademarks have become generic and lost capacity to receive legal protection. By virtue of becoming common names and can be used by competitors and members of the public and hence cannot be protected as a trademark.

268. Trademarks that describe goods or services for which they are applied against are not considered as being capable of distinguishing between different goods and services in the same market. Rather, these trademarks are said to be descriptive. For example, the use of the verb 'drink' on a beverage is considered to be descriptive. Courts in Kenya have held that the word 'Band' is not descriptive of margarine, despite, the trademark, 'Blue Band' being associated with margarine,[127] but 'Pony tail' is descriptive of hair additions, hair pieces, wigs, weaves and braids.[128]

---

123. *Weetabix Ltd. v. Manji Food Industries Ltd.* [2015] eKLR.
124. Trademarks Act, s. 12(2).
125. *Thermos* was declared generic in the case of *King-Seeley Thermos Co v. Aladdin Industries, Inc.* 321 F.2d 577 (2d Cir.1963).
126. The term 'Sellotape' has been defined as a sticky tape; clear plastic that is sticky on one side used for sticking things together. *See* Hornby A.S., *Oxford Advanced Leaner's Dictionary of Current English* Oxford University press (2010).
127. *Unilever PLC v. Bidco Oil Industries* [2004] eKLR.
128. *Strategic Industries Ltd. v. Sana Industries Company Ltd.* [2017] eKLR.

§4. Formalities (Procedure for Obtaining Protection, Establishing and Maintaining Trademarks)

269. Section 4 of the Act establishes the Register of Trade Marks for purposes of registration of trademarks and related activities regarding those trademarks.[129] The Registrar of Trade Marks has the custody, control and management of the register at all times.[130]

270. Registration can be undertaken nationally, regionally or internationally but must be in compliance with the requirements of the Trade Marks Act and Trade Mark Rules made thereunder.

271. The requirements for registration of a trademark are as follows:

- The mark must be formally represented in print format.
- The representation must be original and not copies.
- Where the mark includes words or symbols in any other language other than English, a translation or transliteration as the case may be must be provided.
- A description of the goods and or services for which the trademark is used or proposed to be used. The description should be in accordance with the Nice Classification or the Vienna Agreement as the case may be.

272. It is notable that not all marks which satisfy the above requirements can be registered. The following are prohibited matter and are not registrable as trademarks in Kenya:

- Protected emblems or representations within the meaning of section 2 of the National Flags, Emblems and Names Act.
- Any representations of Heads of States.
- Signs or representations of international organisations such as Red Cross/ Crescent sign.
- Flags, insignias, decorations of flags; abbreviations of titles of any foreign State.
- The Olympic symbol.[131]
- Any trademark that is deceptive, confusing, contrary to law or morality or is scandalous.[132]
- Marks which are identical and resembling to already registered marks.[133]

---

129. Such activities include recording changes in the trademark or in ownership through licenses, assignments and mergers.
130. Other powers of the Registrar include receiving and processing the trademarks applications, effecting corrections on the register, hearing and determining opposition and cancellation proceedings amongst others.
131. Section 59 of the Trade Marks Act.
132. Section 14 of the Trade Marks Act.
133. *See* s. 15 of the Trade Marks Act which has been interpreted by the High Court which has set several tests when determining whether or not trademarks resemble each other. *See British American*

– Marks that are similar or identical to well-known trademarks.[134]

§5. Ownership and Transfer (Assignment: Licenses)

273. Under section 31 of the Trade Marks Act, a person may be registered as a licensee of a trademark in respect of any or all of the goods for which it is registered. To be registered as a licensee, a person must be proposed and thereafter, the proprietor and the proposed licensee must apply in writing to the Registrar of Trade Marks in the prescribed manner[135] together with a statutory declaration by the proprietor, or a duly appointed agent approved by the Registrar. The Registrar may register the proposed licensee if the statutory requirements are met, subject to any restrictions and conditions that the Registrar thinks proper (including if the proposed license is contrary to the public interest).[136] The Registrar will refuse an application to register the proposed licensee as a user of the trademark if the grant of the application will tend to facilitate trafficking in the trademark. The proprietor of the trademark may apply for modification of a registered license. It should be noted that no assignable or transmissible right is permitted to be granted by way of license.[137]

274. The rights of the licensee are limited. Ordinarily the scope of the rights of the licensee will be outlined in the statutory declaration, e.g., terms of the license such as duration and scope. The limited nature of the rights of the licensee were stated by Mutava J in *Twiga Chemical Industries Ltd v. Rotam Ltd & Another,*[138] where the judge stated that the Trademarks Act limited the rights of the licensee to the use of the trademark of the proprietor and not the right to claim ownership in the mark distinctly from the right. Licensees have certain rights even in the absence of a grant of such right in the license. For example, the licensee has the right to institute legal proceedings against a potential infringer if the proprietor neglects or refuses to do so within two months of a request for such enforcement. A licensee also has the power to request the Registrar to correct any error, or change any name, address or description of the trademark.[139]

275. The Registrar may cancel the registration of a mark upon application (in writing) by the proprietor or a licensee on any of the following grounds: that the licensee has used the trademark otherwise than as permitted; that the proprietor or

---

Tobacco Kenya Ltd. v. Cut Tobacco Kenya Ltd. CA 278 of 2008, *Glaxo Group Ltd. v. Syner-Med Pharmaceuticals Ltd.* [2010] eKLR & Beiersdorf *AG v. Emirchem Products Ltd.* (2001) 1KLR 876.

134. *See Weetabix Ltd. v. Manji Foods Industries Ltd.* Civil Case 53 of [2013] eKLR for definition of well known marks in Kenya.

135. Rule 95, *Trade Mark Rules 1956*, provide that the application should be made in Form TM 48.

136. *Ibid.*, s. 31(5).

137. *Ibid.*, s. 31(12).

138. Milimani HCCC No. 447 of 2011 para. 18, quoted in *Bky Insurance Agencies Ltd. v. First Assurance Ltd.* [2013] eKLR.

139. Section 37, *Trade Marks Act* Cap. 506 Laws of Kenya.

the licensee misrepresented or failed to disclose a material fact to the application for registration; that the registration ought not to have been effected having regard to rights vested in the applicant by virtue of a contract in the performance of which he is interested.[140] The Registrar may also cancel the registration of a licensee in respect of a mark that is no longer registered.[141] Such decisions and all other decisions of the Registrar are subject to appeal lodged before the High Court.[142]

§6. Scope of Exclusive Rights

276. Once registered, a trademark proprietor enjoys the following rights:

- The exclusive use of the mark in Kenya in regard to the goods and/or services which the registration covers.
- The right to license or assign part or whole of the trademark to third parties.
- The right to prevent any unauthorised use by third parties of the trademark or trademarks that nearly resemble the registered trademark.[143]
- The right to institute proceedings to prevent and or recover damages for the infringement of the trademark.[144]

277. The above rights are all limited to the extent of the entry contained in the Register of Trade Marks in terms of conditions or limitations registered against the trademark. It is however notable that the above rights especially the right of a trademark owner of preventing unauthorised use or recovering damages that arise out of passing off is not affected by registration.[145]

§7. Limitations of the Scope of Trademark Protection

278. The scope of exclusive rights granted is subject to limitations that fall into two broad categories. The first category relates to those limitations that may be entered into the register. These limitations may include a disclaimer to the exclusive use of a part of a mark, such as word or number, separately and apart from the mark as whole. The second category falls within the prescriptions of sections 10 and 11 of the Trade Marks Act (Cap. 506). Here, a proprietor of a registered mark cannot restrain use by any person of a trademark identical to or nearly resembling the registered mark, in relation to goods to services for which there has been a continued use prior to registration. Similarly, the registration of a trademark shall not interfere with any bona fide use by a person of his own name or the name of his place of business, or of his predecessor's name or his predecessor's place of business, or any bona fide description of the character or quality of goods or services.

---

140. Section 31(8), *Trade Marks Act* Cap. 506 Laws of Kenya.
141. *Ibid.*
142. *Ibid.*, s. 31(11).
143. Section 7 of the Trade Marks Act.
144. Section 5 of the Trade Marks Act.
145. *Ibid.*

279. In *Solpia Kenya Limited v. Style Industries Limited & another*[146] the court affirmed the value of the limitation of the scope of rights on account of prior use of identical or nearly resembling marks. In this case, the court held that, '*where section 10 is called into play, the court should be careful not to use the fact of registration of trade mark as the sole basis of restraining the use of the trade mark by the person claiming prior use of the trade mark.*'

280. With respect to bona fide use by a person of his own name or the name of his place of business the court has stated that the purpose of section 11 is to bar the registration of a trade mark that might infringe on an existing name of a person including a company.[147] Further, goodwill acquired in connection to goods or services in the market for the use of the name in question also appears to count in determination of application of the provision in limiting trademark rights.

§8. Use Requirements

281. Using a trademark following registration is an important condition that the registered proprietor of a trademark must fulfil in order for the trademark to be maintained in the register. A third party can therefore apply for the removal of a trademark from the register on the ground of non-use, either on account of the trademark having been registered without any bona fide intention or bona fide use on the part of the applicant to use it in relation to the goods and services or, for a continuous period of five years, following registration, there has been no bona fide use of the mark by the proprietor.[148]

282. A number of limitations that have been put in place which enable a registered proprietor to escape the 'use' requirements as provided. These are as follows:

- Bona fide use of the trademark by the proprietor in relation to good or services in question.
- Non-use due to special circumstances in relation to goods, or in relation to particular services and not to any intention to abandon the trademark to which the application relates.[149]
- Registration of well-known marks and defensive marks.[150]
- Proposed use of a trademark by a corporation to be constituted.[151]
- Where prove of use is required, such use with addition as and alterations not substantially affecting the identity of a trademark;[152] and

146. [2015] eKLR.
147. *National Industrial Credit (NIC) Bank Ltd. v. Nairobi Investment Company (NIC) Micro Finance Ltd.* [2012] eKLR.
148. Trade Marks Act, s. 29(1).
149. Trade Marks Act, s. 29(3).
150. Trade Marks Act, s. 30.
151. Trade Marks Act, s. 32.
152. Trade Marks Act, s. 33.

– Use of trademark in export trade.[153]

§9. Duration of Protection: Renewal – Termination

283. The duration for registration of a trademark in Kenya is a period of ten years.[154] This duration is renewable for a period of ten years from the date of expiration of the original registration or of the last renewal of registration, as the case may be.[155] Registration and renewal, is subject to fulfilment of the conditions as may be set as well as payment of the requisite fees.

§10. Infringement and Remedies

I. Infringement

284. Infringement of a trademark refers to any use of a registered trademark or a confusingly similar mark to a registered trademark by a third party without the authority of the registered proprietor.

285. Section 7 of the Trade Marks Act defines infringement in the following terms:

> Use, by any person not being the proprietor of the trademark or registered user thereof; of an identical mark or a mark so resembling a registered trademark as to be likely to deceive or cause confusion in the course of trade or in connection with provision of services of which it is registered and in such a manner as to render the mark likely to be taken as being used as a trademark by the proprietor of the trademark or to cause injury to the proprietor of the mark or his licensees.

286. Besides the aforementioned definition of what constitutes infringement of trademarks, the Ant-Counterfeit Act, 2008 also consider trademarks infringement from a counterfeiting perspective, essentially listing a number of actions that a person may take without the authority of an owner of an IPR. With respect to trademarks, the following two actions constitute counterfeiting, and therefore infringement:

– the manufacture, production, packaging, re-packaging, labelling or making, whether in Kenya, of any goods whereby those goods are imitated in such manner and to such a degree that those other goods are identical or substantially similar copies of the goods;

153. Trade Marks Act, s. 34.
154. Trade Marks Act, s. 23(1).
155. Trade Marks Act, s. 23(2).

- the manufacture, production or making, whether in Kenya or elsewhere, the subject matter of a trademark, or a colourable imitation thereof so that the other goods are calculated to be confused with or to be taken as being the goods of the trademark owner or any goods manufactured, produced or made under his licence.

287. For an action to amount to infringement under the Trade Marks Act, there must be a registered trademark, the use must be by an unauthorised person and it must (or be likely to) cause injury to the proprietor of the trademark. However, with respect to counterfeiting, the only requirement for an action to constitute an infringement is taking a listed action without the authority of the trademark owner. Actions for infringement referred to under the Trade Marks Act, and counterfeiting extend only to persons who are registered proprietors of trademarks.

288. A further action that a registered proprietor of a trademark may raise is that of passing off.[156] The Trade Marks Act does not lay the ground for an action for passing off. However, Kenya courts in several decisions such as *Pastificio Lucio Garofalo S.P.A v. Debenham & Fear (2013) Limited;*[157] *Strategic Industries Limited v. Solpia Kenya Limited*[158] and *National Industrial Credit (NIC) Bank Ltd v. Nairobi Investment Company (NIC) Micro Finance Ltd*[159] have adopted the components of passing off as laid down in courts in England, starting in *A.G. Spalding Brothers v. AW Gamage Ltd & Another,*[160] and later in *Reckitt & Colman Products Ltd v. Borden Inc.*[161] In this case, the House of Lords set the test of passing off to be:

- There must be some misrepresentation of a trader's trademark.
- The misrepresentation must be by a trader and in the course of trade.
- The misrepresentation must be to prospective consumers of the trader or ultimate customers of goods and services supplied by the trader.
- The misrepresentation must have been calculated to cause injury to the business or goodwill of the business of the other trader (in the sense that this is a reasonably foreseeable consequence); and
- The misrepresentation must cause actual damage to the business or to the goodwill of the trader by whom the action is brought (or in a quia timet action), will probably do.

289. The aforementioned ingredients for an action for passing off have been adopted by Kenya Courts in several decisions and they now constitute a part of Kenya law.

156. Trade Marks Act, s. 5. An action for passing off is also available to unregistered proprietors of trademarks, unlike actions for infringement and counterfeiting which are not available to them.
157. [2013] eKLR.
158. [2019] eKLR.
159. [2012] eKLR.
160. (1914–1915) All E.R Rep 147; (1915) 32 RPC 237 HL.
161. (1990) 1 All. E.R 873.

II. Remedies

290. Trademarks rights are private rights and the rights holder has to institute proceedings to enforce them. Infringement cases are determined on a balance of probabilities and therefore dependent on the facts presented by the parties. The production of a registration certificate is deemed to be prima facie proof of ownership and validity of the trademark so registered.[162]

291. Under the Trade Marks Act (Cap. 506), the key remedies that are available in infringement cases are injunctions and damages.

292. With respect to injunctions, these may be issued temporarily or at the interlocutory stage, pending the hearing and determination of a suit and also permanently, upon conclusion of a suit. Where an injunction is sought at an interlocutory stage, the plaintiff must satisfy the following conditions as laid out in *Giella v. Cassman Brown & Co Ltd*:[163]

- A prima facie case must be made out by the plaintiff.
- The plaintiff must demonstrate that he stands to suffer irreparable harm which would not adequately be compensated by award for damages.
- The balance of convenience favours the grant of an injunction.

293. The three conditions stated are often cited when temporary injunctions are sought in trademarks cases.[164]

294. The principles applicable in assessment of damages as set out in *Gerber v. Lectra,*[165] are binding in Kenyan courts, having been applied in various cases.[166] Therefore:

- Damages are compensatory only, to put the claimant in the same position he would have been in had the wrong not been sustained.
- The burden of proof lies on the claimant, but damages are to be assessed liberally.
- Where the claimant has licensed his rights, the damages are the lost royalty.
- It is irrelevant that the defendant could have competed lawfully; and
- Where the claimant has exploited his right by his own sales, he can claim lost profit on sales by the defendant he would have made otherwise, and lost profit on his own sales to the extent that he was forced by the infringement to reduce his own price.

295. Injunctions and damages are also available for actions of passing off.

---

162. *See* ss 16 and 46 of the Trade Marks Act.
163. (1973)EA 358.
164. *See* for example, *Olx B.V v. Radio Africa Ltd.* [2017] eKLR; *Colour Planet Ltd. v. Safaricom Ltd. & 2 others* [2016] eKLR.
165. (1995) R.P.C.383.
166. *See Pastificio Lucio Garofalo S.P.A v. Debenham & Fear (2013) Ltd.* [2013] eKLR.

296. An additional remedy that is available is an account of profits. This is an equitable remedy and the court has discretion to grant it or not. The principles that English courts have set out in applications for accounts for profits[167] are now binding, as Kenya courts have adopted them in rendering local decisions. These principles are:

- An account is confined to the accounts actually made, its purpose being to deprive the defendant of unjust enrichment rather than to punish him.
- An account is addressed to identifying profits caused, in the legal sense, by the infringement.
- The fact that the defendant's profits could have been in a non-infringing fashion is irrelevant.
- The claimant must take the defendant as he finds him, and may not argue that the defendant could have made greater profits by trading in a different fashion.
- Where only parts of the defendant's activities infringed, profits attributable to the non-infringing parts are not caused by the infringement, and the overall profits must be apportioned.

297. The Anti-Counterfeit Act (2008) provides for a route through which a trademark owner, where his goods are being counterfeited may lay criminal complaints against the counterfeiter. This statute therefore criminalises certain acts in relation to counterfeit goods.[168] These actions include:

- Possession.
- Manufacture and production.
- Selling, hiring, barter or exchanging, offering for sale or exposing for sale.
- Exposing and exhibiting for the purposes of sale.
- Distribution; and
- Importation, transhipping and exporting.

298. Besides criminalisation of the aforementioned actions where upon being found guilty one may be convicted for up to three years or fined up to KES 2 million, other remedies available include seizure, detention, destruction[169] and stoppage of manufacturing of counterfeit goods and anti-counterfeit inspectors and authorised officers.

167. These principles are laid out in *My Kinda Town v. Soll [1982] F.S.R*, *Celanese v. BP [1999] RPC 203* and in *Dart v. Décor [1994] FSR 567.*

168. Anti-counterfeit Act, s. 32.

169. *Kitale CMCC No. 3268 of 2014 R v. Ahmed Hassan*, the court ordered for the destruction of twenty-three counterfeit phones.

Chapter 5. Tradenames

§1. Sources – Legislation

299. Legal provisions on tradenames are scattered throughout several pieces of legislations in Kenya that govern registration of tradenames, either as corporate names or as business names, whether by corporations, individuals, firms, partnerships, trusts or non-governmental organisations.

300. Registration of tradenames is not a unified function inasmuch as the law establishes the Business Registration Service.[170] The functions of the Business Registration Service is to implement policies, laws and other matters relating to the registration of companies, partnerships and firms, individuals and corporations carrying on business under a business name, bankruptcy, hire-purchase, and security rights.[171] The service also maintains registers, data and records on registrations carried out by it. The above notwithstanding, the Business Registration Service is involved in the registration of certain tradenames and business names, but not all. Tradenames concerning societies, trusts and public benefit organisations do not fall under the purview of the Business Registration Service.

301. The following statutes thus govern tradenames and business names in some way or other, particularly in providing that entities or firms regulated under these statutes must be registered, thereby conferred with protection:

- Banking Act (Cap. 488).
- Business Registration Service Act (2015).
- Companies Act (2015).
- Co-operative Societies Act (1997).
- Limited Liability Partnership Act (2011).
- Partnerships Act (2012).
- Public Benefits Organisations Act (2013).
- Registration of Business Names Act (Cap. 499).
- Trustee Act (Cap. 167).
- Trustee (Perpetual Succession Act) (Cap. 164).

§2. The Protection of Trade Names

302. Kenya law does not specifically distinguish between tradenames and business names. Whereas a business name is defined,[172] a tradename is not. However, a

170. Business Registration Service Act (2015).
171. *Ibid.*, s. 4.
172. According to s. 2 of the Registration of Business Names (Cap.499), a 'business name' means the name or style under which any business (every trade, occupation or profession) is carried on, whether in partnership or otherwise.

tradename is generally recognised as a name by which an individual, firm or corporate entity may be trading as, including its own name. Therefore, the difference between a business name and a tradename appears to be whether the name in which an individual, firm or corporate entity is trading by is its own name or other.

303. The general principle is that for a tradename or a business name to be protected, it must be registered, and the protection that arises is that the registering authority is thereafter empowered not to cause a name similar to the tradename already in the register to be registered. It is notable that the Companies Act (2015) is explicit in this regard, by prohibiting the Registrar from registering a company by a name that is the same as another name appearing in the index of company names.[173] It therefore follows that being 'first to register' is an important element in conferring protection, as opposed to being 'first to use'.

304. Under Kenyan law, registration of certain business names is mandatory. According to section 4 of the Registration of Business Names Act (Cap. 499), registration of business name is mandatory where:

- a firm having a place of business in Kenya and carrying on business under a business name which does not consist of the surnames of all individuals who are partners and the corporate names of all corporations which are partners, without any addition other than the forenames of individual partners or the initials of such forenames.
- an individual having a place of business in Kenya and carrying on business under a business name which does not consist of his surname without any addition other than his forenames or the initials thereof.
- an individual or firm having a place of business in Kenya, who, or a member of which, has either changed his name, otherwise than, in the case of a woman, in consequence of marriage.
- a corporation having a place of business in Kenya and carrying on business under a business name which does not consist of its corporate name without any addition.

305. However, registration is not necessary in the following instances:

- where two or more individual partners have the same surname, the addition of an 's' at the end of that surname does not render registration of the business name to be necessary;
- where the business is carried on by a trustee in bankruptcy or by a receiver or manager appointed by the court;
- in a purchase or acquisition of property by two or more persons as joint tenants or tenants in common, whether or not the owner shares any profits arising from the sale thereof.

173. Companies Act (2015), s. 57(1).

306. With respect to tradenames of companies, the Companies Act (2015) provides several strict provisions with respect to their registration, and prohibits registration of the following:

- use of the name would constitute an offence;[174]
- use of offensive or undesirable names;
- use of a name suggesting connection with the State or local or public authority.[175]

307. Further, regulations may prohibit the use of specified characters, signs or symbols when appearing in specified positions in a name.[176]

308. Company names are required to indicate the company type. Thus:

- A company that is both a limited company and a public company may only be registered with a name that ends with the words 'public limited company' or the abbreviation 'plc'.[177]
- A company that is both a limited company and private company may be registered only with a name that ends with the word 'limited' or the abbreviation 'ltd'.[178] However, the Cabinet Secretary may, by notice given to the company, exempt a private company from using the word 'limited' or 'Ltd'.[179] Companies limited by guarantee are normally exempted from using the words 'limited' or 'Ltd' following incorporation.

309. The Companies Act (2015) confers powers upon the Registrar to cause names of companies to be changed under certain cases. These include instances where the name of a company is the same or too similar to a name either appearing at the time of the registration, or should have appeared in the Registrar's index of company names.[180] Kenyan courts have followed the precedent set in the UK in *Leny v. Walker [1879] 10 ch D.P 206*[181] in this regard. Thus in *Republic v. Registrar of Companies & another* Ex parte *Atlantic Group (K) Limited*[182] the High Court in judicial review applied the principles set out in the *Leny case* in finding that the

174. Companies Act (2015), s. 49.
175. *Ibid.*, s. 50.
176. *Ibid.*, s. 52.
177. *Ibid.*, s. 53.
178. *Ibid.*, s. 54.
179. *Ibid.*, s. 55.
180. *Ibid.*, s. 58(1).
181. In this English case, it was expounded that, 'These provisions are designed principally to prevent similar names getting to the register, but the registration of a company by a name which is calculated to deceive by reason of its identity with or resemblance to the name used by some other registered company ... will not prevent the courts from intervening in a proper case by injunction, to protect the rights of such last mentioned company for the court has jurisdiction to restrain a defendant from using a trade name colourably resembling that of the plaintiff, if the defendant's trade name though innocently adopted is calculated to deceive either: by diverting customers from the plaintiff to the defendants, or by occasioning confusion between the two businesses'.
182. Nairobi JR. Miscellaneous Application No. 329 of 2016.

provisions of sections 15,16,19 and 20 of the Companies Act (cap. 486) (now repealed), were designed to prevent similar names getting to the register.

310. Good faith or inadvertent registration is not a defence to prevent the Registrar from exercising his powers to cause a change in the name of a company where similarity of names arises. In *Republic v. Registrar of Companies ex parte Trans-global Freight Logistics Limited and Global Freight Logistics Limited*[183] the court said:

> *The fact of registration through 'inadvertence or otherwise', carries with it good faith, but also many sins of commission and omission. How does the Registrar discover that a company has been registered inadvertently or otherwise? He or she does so by own research on the index of companies, or on notice by an Interested Party.*

311. The Registrar may also cause names of companies to change where misleading information was given for registration of a company[184] or where the name of a company gives misleading indication of its activities.[185]

312. The above provisions notwithstanding, the strength of protection conferred to a registered tradename or a business name is not similar to that conferred to a tradename or business name when registered as a trademark. In *Hamdi Restaurant Limited v. Hamdi Hotels and Restaurant Limited & another*[186] parties were contesting over registration of different tradenames under the Companies Act, both containing the name, ***'HAMDI'***. In this case, the High Court found the plaintiff to have no legal basis to lay claim over the name or word ***'HAMDI'*** yet they had not registered the same as a trademark. Similarly, in *Agility Logistics Ltd & 2 Others v. Agility Logistics Kenya Ltd*[187] the court made the following observations on the Companies Act (2015) and the Trademarks Act (Cap. 506):

> My take on the two pieces of legislation is that whereas the Companies Act governs registration of company names, the fact of registration per se does not extend protection to the name of the company itself as does the protection provided by a trademark. The Companies Act only protects such names to the extent that no other can be registered by a similar name but does not protect the intellectual property in the name itself as to confer exclusive use, as does a trademark.

183. Misc. Application No. 711 of 2005.
184. Companies Act (2015), s. 60.
185. *Ibid.* Also *see* the decision in *Leny v. Walker* [1879] 10 ch D.P 206.
186. [2014] eKLR.
187. [2012] eKLR.

313. Courts have followed a similar principle on the strength of business names conferred protection under the Registration of Business Names Act (Cap. 499). In *P.M.Macharia t/a Batian Guest Hotel v. Batian Grand Hotel Limited*,[188] the High Court stated:

> The position in law is that the registration of a business name per se under the Registration of Business Names Act and/or the Companies Act does not extend protection of the name in the same way that protection is extended to registered marks under the Trade Marks Act (Act No. 4 of 2002).

188. [2018] eKLR.

Chapter 6. Industrial Designs

314. Industrial Designs represent an aspect of IP law that was, for a great long while, underutilised and often considered to be of less importance than certain other forms of IPR. Consider that, in the United States as of January 2015, fewer than 80,000 design patents the equivalent to industrial designs in the U.S. had been granted as compared with roughly nine million utility patents. Year on year since 1990, the number of utility patent applications in the United States is consistently more than fifteen times the number of design patent applications.

315. Not everyone eschewed industrial designs: some industries such as fashion, automobiles, and packaging have used this form of IPR extensively. The design patent for the Coca Cola bottle[189] is perhaps the most iconic of all design patents, and the design itself is known and recognised throughout the world. Furthermore, the dominance of utility patents is not the case in Kenya, where the number of granted industrial designs is actually greater than the number of granted patents.

316. Internationally, any obscurity of industrial designs all but disappeared when Apple, Inc. sued Samsung Electronics Company in 2011 over several utility patents and design patents owned by Apple. The ensuing 'smart phone wars' helped to expose the importance of design, even for products that typically outlive their useful life every few years. Initial successes in the lawsuits by Apple demonstrated to the massive electronics industry that industrial designs are, in fact, valuable IPR. Indeed, since 2010, the rate of growth in design patent applications in the U.S. has outpaced the rate of growth in utility patent applications. *See* Figure 3.

189. *See* USD 105,529, granted in 1937.

Figure 3 Year-on-Year Number of Applications for Utility Patents and Design Patents[190]

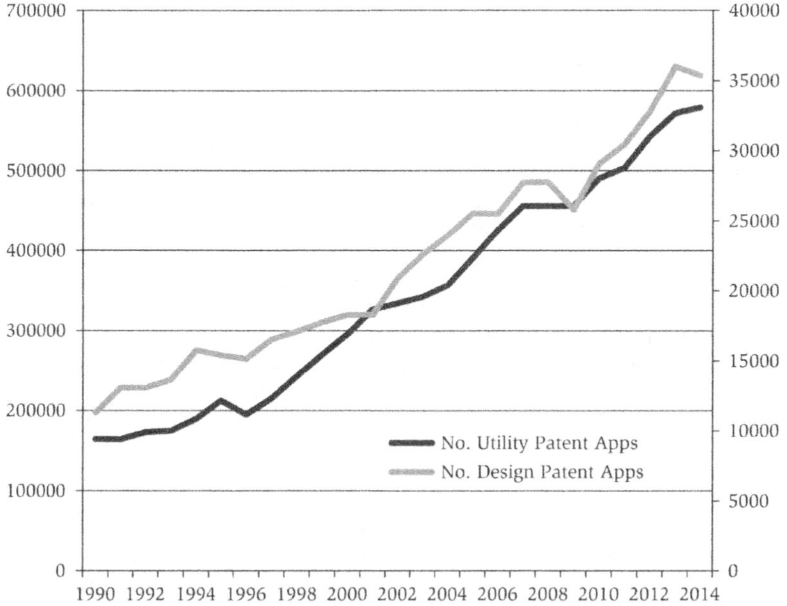

317. With confusing similarities to both copyright law and patent law, industrial designs remain poorly understood by some IP practitioners and applicants. Even the name of this IPR can be confusing – in some countries they are known as design patents, in other countries industrial designs – and applying the principles of the relevant law is not always straight forward.

318. This chapter provides an introduction to industrial designs, with a special emphasis on distinguishing industrial designs from copyrights and patents.

§1. Sources – Legislation

319. Industrial designs in Kenya are provided by the IPA 2001, Part XIII. This relatively short Part of the IPA 2001 consists of just 10 sections, plus incorporation by reference of several other sections of the IPA 2001 concerning licensing and ownership.

190. Source: United States Patent and Trademark Office website.

320. Industrial designs granted by the ARIPO, provided that Kenya is a designated state in the industrial design, have the same effect as a nationally granted industrial design.

§2. Subject Matter of Protection

321. Industrial designs are defined as 'any composition of lines or colours or any three-dimensional form, whether or not associated with lines or colours: Provided that such composition or form gives a special appearance to a product of industry or handicraft and can serve as a pattern for a product of industry or handicraft.'[191] Several aspects of this definition require further comment.

322. By the statutory definition, industrial designs apply to designs that are in two dimensions as well as designs in three dimensions. This is evident from the use of the alternative: protection is for any composition of lines or colours *or* any three-dimensional form. Designs in three dimensions are intuitive and need little explanation – everyday objects from beverage cups and bottles to hats and helmets exist in three dimensions, and the protected aspects of such objects focus on their three-dimensional shape. Two-dimensional designs are less intuitive, and there is no guidance from the IPA. Nevertheless, two-dimensional designs likely include lines and colours forming designs on paper, disposed on surfaces, including on surfaces that form a three-dimensional shape, such as lines or colours on a bottle, and in electronic form. The latter category, in many jurisdictions, is useful for protecting computer icons and website designs, among other electronic designs. For example, the original Google homepage with a search bar and two buttons was design patented in the United States.[192]

323. The second aspect of the statutory definition worth mentioning is the protected design must give a 'special appearance' to a product. Again, the IPA does not give further guidance for defining a special appearance, and it is not clear how this limitation differs from the requirement that a design be 'new' (*see* below). In practice, the bar for a special appearance tends to be quite low, provided that the design satisfies other statutory criteria.

§3. Conditions of Protection

324. In addition to the definition, industrial designs are further limited by a novelty requirement. The requirement is similar to the novelty requirement for patents and UMCs, with an important exception. Whereas the 'new' requirement for patents is strictly worldwide regardless of the form of prior disclosure, the 'new' requirement for designs is worldwide only for disclosures to the public in tangible

191. Industrial Property Act 2001, s. 84(1).
192. *See* USD 599,372, granted in 2009.

form. Use of the design, where such use is made outside of Kenya, does not constitute a novelty-destroying activity with respect to industrial designs.

§4. Formalities (Procedure for Grant and Obtaining Protection)

325. Registration is required in order to obtain an industrial design. Registration involves an application made to the KIPI. The application contains one or more graphic representations that show the design for which protection is sought. In Kenya, drawings and photographs are explicitly allowed forms of such graphic representations. The most typical approach in an application contains seven drawings – one each showing the top, bottom, left, right, front, and back views of the object, and a seventh drawing showing an isometric view. The application may include a single claim that makes reference to the drawings. Furthermore, the application should be accompanied by a specimen of the object.[193]

326. Upon receipt of an application, KIPI is required to substantively examine the application to ensure that the design satisfies the novelty requirement and that the design is not purely for function. Unlike patents, there is no minimum waiting period after filing an application before the industrial design application can be examined and granted. Upon grant, the application is published – i.e., laid open to the public – in the Industrial Property Journal.

327. As with patents and UMCs, the IPA 2001 provides[194] that any member of the public can initiate revocation proceedings for a published industrial design, provided that such proceedings are initiated within nine months of the publication date.

§5. Ownership and Transfer (Assignment: Licenses)

328. *See* Chapter 2, patents.

§6. Scope of Exclusive Rights

329. The rights provided by industrial design protection are the exclusive right to sell for commercial or industrial purposes goods in which the design is incorporated.[195] In addition the industrial design registration provides the patent-like rights of reproducing the industrial design in the manufacture of a product, importing a product reproducing the protected design, and stocking, selling or offering for sale

193. Industrial Property Act 2001, s. 87.
194. Industrial Property Act 2001, s. 103(2).
195. Industrial Property Act 2001, s. 85(1).

such a product.[196] Induced liability is specifically provided: an owner of an industrial design may bring suit against anyone who actually infringes the protected design as well as anyone 'who performs acts which make it likely that infringement will occur.'[197]

§7. Limitations of the Scope of Protection

330. An important qualification on the definition of industrial designs is that protection cannot extend to 'anything in an industrial design which serves solely to obtain a technical result.'[198] This limitation is critical as it firmly places industrial design protection on the *design* of an object rather than, as with patents, the *function* of an object. Perhaps the most challenging aspect of industrial designs, however, is determining when a feature of a design serves solely to obtain a technical result.

331. Consider the iconic Coca Cola bottle, mentioned above and protected by a design patent in the United States. Is the design of the bottle purely aesthetic, purely for achieving a technical result, or some combination of the two? Note that the discussion centres on the appearance of the bottle – i.e., the combination of lines and colours that form the object. Other aspects of the bottle such as the material from which the bottle is made, any trademarks that are displayed on the bottle, etc., are not part of the analysis. Obviously there is at least *some* aspect of an aesthetic design in the shape of the bottle, since the shape of the bottle is recognised throughout the world. However it cannot be said that the bottle shape is without function. For example, Coca Cola bottles have roughly an hourglass shape that enables a consumer to grasp the bottle more comfortably just below the vertical centreline. The bulge above the centreline is important because it prevents the bottle, which may be slippery when wet from condensation, from slipping out of the consumer's hand. The vertical ribbing also improves the ability of the consumer to grasp the bottle. Clearly, then, there are functional aspects of the bottle's shape, as well as aesthetic aspects. The shape of the bottle remains suitable for design protection, however, provided that such features are not solely for obtaining a technical result.

332. Notwithstanding the prohibition on coverage of elements that serve solely to obtain a technical result, industrial designs are limited to designs of products of industry or handicrafts. This removes purely artistic works such as paintings and sculptures (other than handicrafts) from the scope of industrial design protection. Technical drawings and similar works for products of industry may be covered by design protection, and in some cases simultaneously covered by copyright.

196. Industrial Property Act 2001, s. 92.
197. Industrial Property Act 2001, s. 92(3).
198. Industrial Property Act 2001, s. 84(2).

§8. Duration of Protection

333. Registered industrial designs are valid for an initial five-year term. Upon payment of appropriate fees, the term may be extended for up to two additional consecutive five-year terms.

§9. Infringement and Remedies

334. Various standards are possible for determining whether a product infringes a valid registered industrial design. In most jurisdictions the product need not be exactly like the drawings provided in the industrial design document – some variations are allowed and only where there is significant deviation will there be a finding of non-infringement. In some jurisdictions, an object will be infringing if it has the same look and feel as the drawings in a granted industrial design. Kenyan case law, which is discussed below, generally follows this latter standard.

I. Case Law

335. The majority of Kenya High Court cases relating to industrial designs merely address procedural issues rather than substantive issues. One exception is the case of *ENG Kenya Ltd v. Magnate Ventures Ltd.*[199] The plaintiff applied to the KIPI for an industrial design for a suburban sign. The application was accepted and a publication of the same put in the Industrial Property Journal. The publication was intended to invite, if any, opposition by the public to the registration of the design but no opposition was filed. As the plaintiff awaited the grant of the industrial design, it began to use the suburban design. A month and a half later, the defendant copied the same. The plaintiff then applied to the court for an interlocutory and a mandatory injunction to restrain the defendant. The issues for the High Court were whether the plaintiff had a right to institute the suit for an advertised industrial design during the nine months within which revocation proceedings may be initiated, and whether the defendant's act infringed any right of the plaintiff. The court held that the plaintiff had a right to institute proceedings pursuant to section 55(c)(ii) vesting a claim for compensation where one has used the subject matter of a published application without the applicant's authorisation. The court examined the two suburban signs and found that they were similar. It held that the defendant had copied the plaintiff's design in order to cause confusion in the market before the plaintiff's design was formally registered. The court issued an interlocutory injunction restraining the defendant from using the design and a mandatory injunction directing the defendant to bring down all the signs it had erected which were similar to those of the plaintiff. The respondent appealed to the Court of Appeal[200] but the application was dismissed.

---

199. *ENG Kenya Ltd. v. Magnate Ventures Ltd.* [2009] eKLR.
200. *Magnate Ventures Ltd. v. Eng Kenya Ltd.* [2009] eKLR.

336. A second example is the case of *Safepak Ltd. v. General Plastics Ltd.*[201] In this case the appellant filed an application challenging the decision of the IPT allowing the Respondent time to put in more evidence material.[202] The additional evidence was intended to show that the industrial design registered to the Appellant should not have been issued since it was already a design in the public domain. In staying the proceedings of the Tribunal pending the determination of the matter, the court observed that while the Respondent was legally entitled to challenge the propriety of the registration of the design and was doing so, the proceedings were not finalised and the protection arising from the registration was still intact. The Court stated that such protection lasts until the industrial design is revoked.

337. In *Friendship Container Mfr. Ltd. v. Yash Plastomet Pvt. Ltd,*[203] the IPT held that it did not have the authority under the IPA 2001 to extend the nine-month period within which the Applicant was able to file revocation proceedings for a granted/published industrial design.

§10. Overlapping and Relation to Other IP Laws

338. Industrial designs can, and frequently do, exist side by side with other IPR for a single product. Those other IPR are typically copyright, patents, and trademarks.

I. Copyright

339. Copyright law in Kenya provides protection for artistic works, which is defined to include sculptures as well as 'works of artistic craftsmanship, pictorial woven tissues and articles of applied handicraft and industrial art.'[204] Although such three-dimensional works and handicraft are classified as 'artistic', there is no explicit statement in the copyright law that such works cannot also be functional in nature. Indeed many objects such as lampstands and chairs are as many artistic works as they are articles of manufacture. Accordingly it is conceivable that both copyright law and design law can apply to certain objects or certain components of an object.

340. Even where there is overlap in covered subject matter, copyright and industrial designs differ in a variety of important ways. The most significant differences are three, the first of which duration: copyright protection lasts fifty years after the death of the author, substantially longer than the maximum fifteen years provided by industrial design. Even where the author of a copyrighted work is unknown, the fifty years of protection is more than three times the duration of industrial designs.

---

201. *Safepak Ltd. v. General Plastics Ltd.* [2012] eKLR.
202. *General Plastics Ltd. v. SafePak Ltd.*, Ind. Prop. Trib. No. 16 of 2002.
203. *Friendship Container Mfr. Ltd. v. Yash Plastomet Pvt. Ltd,* Ind. Prop. Trib. No. 54 of 2007.
204. Kenya Copyright Act 2001, s. 2(1).

341. The second critical difference pertains to registration: copyright has no requirements of registration and is automatically granted upon fixation of the work, whereas industrial design protection is only granted upon application to KIPI, and only after KIPI has undertaken substantive examination. Accordingly the number of industrial designs available for enforcement is substantially fewer in number.

342. The third difference is in the international treatment of the right. The reader will recall that, through the Berne Convention, copyright is fairly international inasmuch as a valid copyright that originates in one Berne Convention country is automatically afforded protection in other Berne Convention countries. Individual country-by-country registrations of the copyright are not necessary for the enforceable right. In contrast, industrial designs (like patents and most trademarks) are territorial and are not valid outside of the country of registration.

343. These three important differences lead to a prominent case in the UK, *Lucasfilm v. Ainsworth.*[205] Mr Ainsworth was involved, in the 1970s, with designing the helmets worn by Storm Troopers in the iconic movie Star Wars. Merchandise and souvenirs from the movie were highly collectable, and the helmet was popular among fans of the movie. Mr Ainsworth retained a mould for the helmet, began producing helmet replicas in the UK, and sold the replicas via the Internet as collectable items in the 2000s. Lucasfilm sued over such sales and claimed that the helmets were sculptures and therefore subject to copyright protection. If the helmets were in fact sculptures, copyright protection would extend well beyond the time period in question. In contrast, Mr Ainsworth argued that the helmets were functional and therefore only entitled to industrial design protection. Even if such rights had been applied for and obtained, they would have expired in the early 1990s. The Supreme Court of the UK ruled that the helmets were functional and therefore not subject to copyright protection as sculpture under UK law.[206]

II. Patents

344. Industrial designs and patents are intended to be minimally overlapping. The law of patents requires that a patented feature of a product must have industrial use and be a solution to a technical problem – i.e., it must be functional in nature. The law of industrial designs, in contrast, prohibits protection of anything solely functional. The qualifier 'solely' leaves open the possibility of obtaining design protection for features that are both aesthetic and functional, and as mentioned previously the dividing line can be elusive if not altogether illusory in some cases. Nevertheless, a reasonable initial inquiry when determining whether a feature can/

205. *Lucasfilm Ltd. and others v. Ainsworth and another*, [2011] UKSC 39, [2012] 1 AC 208.
206. The applicable UK law is the Copyright, Designs and Patents Act 1988. Unlike the Kenyan Copyright Act, the UK law explicitly states that copyright cannot extend to functional products.

should be protected with patents versus industrial designs is whether there is a functional purpose, and how significant the functional purpose is to the feature. If numerous other designs could achieve the same or similar function, it is more likely that the design is non-functional.

345. The application, and therefore the scope of protection, is also quite different. A patent disclosure contains thorough textual explanations of the product as well as all variations that achieve the same technical effect. Accordingly, functionally equivalent variations – particularly but not necessarily only those described in the patent specification – are within the scope of protection of a patent. In contrast, industrial design applications contain little or no text, but only images of the protected design. Thus the scope of protection focuses on whether a potentially infringing product has a similar look and feel, rather than any similar functionality.

III. Trademark

346. Recall that a 'mark' as defined in the Kenyan Trademarks Act includes marks rendered in two-dimensional and three-dimensional form, and in relatively rare occasions trademark protection is sought for three-dimensional marks. Similarly, industrial design protection can be obtained for designs rendered in two or three dimensions. Furthermore, both trademarks and industrial designs apply to products with industrial use.

347. Some items may be afforded industrial design protection and trademark protection. Consider the ornaments that are found on the bonnet of some automobiles (e.g., the tri-point star of Mercedes Benz). The ornament is often a three-dimensional replica of the trademark of the automobile manufacturer. Clearly such ornaments are afforded trademark protection. Arguably too, such ornaments are products of industry, and yet the design does not serve solely to obtain a technical result. They are therefore suitable for industrial design protection. These arguments can even be made for two-dimensional ornaments that are disposed flat against the bonnet (e.g., the two coloured circle of BMW), since industrial designs can be obtained for two-dimensional combinations of lines and colours.

348. The primary difference, then, between trademarks and industrial designs is the requirement of distinctiveness for the latter as compared with novelty for the former. Novelty and distinctiveness are quite different concepts that the reader must be capable of distinguishing. Novelty means that a design has not been previously disclosed anywhere in the world to the public, and extends forever backward in time from the filing of an industrial design application. Small differences between prior designs and the new design may be sufficient to satisfy the novelty requirement. In contrast, distinctiveness means that a mark is recognisable so as to indicate the source of a good or service. Distinctiveness does not require that a mark is new – indeed previously used marks that have been out of use for some period of time, as well as marks that are currently in use in other jurisdictions, may obtain trademark protection.

349. Another important difference is duration – trademark protection can be perpetual as long as renewal fees are paid, whereas industrial design protection can be renewed only a maximum of three times.

Chapter 7. Plant Variety Protection

350. Kenya's plant varieties protection (PVP) history can be traced to 1972 when the Seeds and Plant Varieties Act (Cap. 326) Laws of Kenya was enacted. Modelled under the 1964 Plant Varieties and Seeds Act of the UK, the 1972 statute addressed broad issues: seed certification and PVP. The seed certification component of the law was activated immediately upon the statute coming into force. However, the PVP part of the law was not implemented until 1995 with the first application for grant of PVP rights being made in 1999. Since then, the statute has undergone several amendments, with the most recent being the enactment of the Seeds and Plant Varieties (Amendment) Act, 2012.

§1. Sources – Legislation and International Treaties

351. The architecture of registration and grant of PVP in Kenya is laid out under several statutes.

I. The Seeds and Plant Varieties Act, 1972 (Cap. 326) Laws of Kenya

352. This statute laid down the initial framework for registration and grant of PVP. While the statute was enacted in 1972, provisions relating to registration and grant of PVP were not activated until 1995 following the enactment of the Seeds and Plant Varieties (Plant Breeders' Rights) Regulations. These Regulations set to operationalise the framework provided for under this statute. The conditions of grant of PVP and the scope of rights for a breeder under this statute and regulations were crafted to conform to the 1978 Act of the International Convention for the Protection of New Varieties of Plants (UPOV 1978). Kenya had acceded to UPOV 1978 in 1999 with the accession marking the onset for application and granting of PVP.

II. The Seeds and Plant Varieties (Amendment) Act, 2012 (No. 53 of 2012)

353. This statute did not repeal the Seeds and Plant Varieties Act (Cap. 326) in its entirety. Rather this legislation was passed with a view to mainly; upgrade Kenya's PVP architecture to be in consonance with the 1991 Act of the (UPOV 1991). Unlike UPOV 1978, UPOV 1991 expands the scope of rights a plant breeder has over the protected variety. It also limits the exceptions to the rights, such that for a third party to undertake some activities over a protected variety, permission has to be sought from the breeder. The enactment of the Seeds and Plant Varieties (Amendment) Act, 2012 also opened the door for Kenya to accede to UPOV 1991 which it so did in April 2016.

III. The Anti-Counterfeit Act, 2008

354. Anti-Counterfeit Act, 2008 is also a relevant statute in complementing the two PVP statutes in enforcement matters. The statute defines IPR broadly to include PVP.[207] Thereafter, 'counterfeiting' is defined as taking certain actions without the authority of the IPR. This statute also establishes the Anti-Counterfeit Authority as a state agency with powers to criminally prosecute infringers of IPR, and grants customs authorities powers to deal with border matters concerning importation of infringing material.

IV. The Kenya Plant Health Inspectorate Service Act, 2012

355. The Kenya Plant Health Inspectorate Service Act (2012) re-established through statute, the Kenya Plant Health Inspectorate Service (KEPHIS), following the revocation of the KEPHIS Order (1996), a regulation which previously established KEPHIS. KEPHIS is the state agency mandated to among others; administer the law relating to application and grant of PVP. The purpose of re-establishing KEPHIS by statute was to essentially provide it with legal autonomy and independence, as a state corporation and to enable it to undertake expanded functions beyond those conferred to it under the 1996 Order. However, administration of PVP in Kenya and acting as the liaison with the International Union for the Protection of New Varieties of Plants (UPOV) has remained one of its core functions, as well as overseeing seed certification and regulation of the seed industry.

356. With regard to international conventions that are relevant, Kenya is a signatory to those described below.

V. 1991 Act of the International Convention for the Protection of New Varieties (UPOV)

357. The first Act of the UPOV Convention was enacted in 1961 but came into force in 1968. The Convention was subsequently revised by the 1972, 1978 and the 1991 Acts. Kenya signed the 1978 Act 13 May, 1999 and in 2016, ratified the 1991 Act thus superseding the 1978 Act. The 1972 Seeds and Plant Varieties Act was modelled on the earlier version of UPOV Acts. However, the enactment of the Seeds and Plants Varieties (Amendment) Act, 2012 saw the PVP system amended to fall in line with the 1991 Act of UPOV especially on the standards of testing new varieties prior to the issuance of the grants of PVP, and on the rights conferred on a plant breeder upon the grant on PVP.

207. Anti-Counterfeit Act (2008), s. 2.

VI. International Treaty on Plant Genetic Resources for Food and Agriculture (ITPGRFA)

358. The International Treaty on Plant Genetic Resources for Food and Agriculture (ITPGRFA) is a comprehensive treaty whose aim is to guarantee food security through conservation, exchange and sustainable use of the world's plant genetic resources for food and agriculture (PGRFA), and the fair and equitable benefit sharing arising from its use.[208] Kenya is a signatory to this Treaty having ratified it in 2003.[209] However, there is no national law in place to domesticate the provisions of this Treaty, and therefore its implementation is dependent on the provisions of Articles 2(5) and (6) of the Constitution, 2010.

359. The relevance of the Treaty to PVP matters in Kenya lies in the fact that the Treaty among others, establishes a Multilateral System of Access and Benefit-Sharing to facilitate plant germplasm and benefit sharing through Standard Material Transfer Agreement.[210] Thus, plant germplasm for food crops from Kenya does get to be transferred between the parties via the mechanisms established under this Treaty and where commercialised, or PVP taken out, then benefit sharing ought to follow the Treaty provisions.

§2. Subject Matter of Protection

360. The subject matter for grant of PVP is not a plant, but rather, a plant variety. Was it to be that the subject matter for protection is a plant that is, a single plant unit this would mean that essentially, the life of the right would only exist to the extent that the plant itself was in existence and would be distinguished upon the plant ceasing to exist. Furthermore, a plant breeder would be required to register rights in respect of each plant unit produced. This would be an extremely costly and cumbersome affair. For this and other reasons, the subject matter for protection is a plant variety, not a plant.

361. The Seeds and Plant Variety Act, 1972 defines a plant variety to mean, a plant grouping within a single botanical taxon of the lowest known rank, defined by the expression of the characteristics resulting from a given genotype or combination of genotypes distinguished from any other plant grouping by the expression of at least one of the said characteristics and considered as a unit with regard to its suitability for being propagated unchanged.[211] A plant variety is therefore a plant grouping, not a single unit within a single botanical taxon of the lowest known rank. The definition of 'plant variety' as contained in section 2 of the Seeds and Plant Variety

208. Preamble to the ITPGRFA.
209. Kenya acceded to this Convention on the 27 May 2003 but it came into force on 29 Jun. 2004. *See* http://www.fao.org/fileadmin/user_upload/legal/docs/033s-e.pdf.
210. Article 12.4 of the ITPGRFA.
211. The Seeds and Plant varieties Act (1972), s. 2.

Act, 1972 is adopted from what is widely accepted to be the definition, even as contained in the various Acts of the UPOV Convention.

§3. CONDITIONS OF PROTECTION

362. The Seeds and Plant Varieties Act, 1972 and the Seeds and Plant Varieties (Amendment) Act, 2012, set four conditions that have to be fulfilled in order for a grant of PVP to be made to an applicant. These conditions are that the variety for which an application is made must be (1) new (2) distinct (3) uniform (4) stable. The conditions for grant as set out in the statutes are a domestication of the international requirements for grant, which are well laid out in all UPOV Conventions.

I. New

363. A variety is considered new under the Kenyan PVP law if as at the date of filing of the application for PVP, propagating or harvested material of the variety has not been sold or otherwise disposed of to others with the consent of the owner for purposes of exploitation.[212] The flexibility also extends to the time of exploitation, and in Kenya the variety must not have been sold or disposed one year prior to the application or four years outside Kenya.[213] The applicant is also expected to declare and confirm whether and for how long the variety has previously been sold, exhibited or otherwise released or exploited in Kenya.

364. A variety is considered to have been released to the market if it had been exhibited in a symposium for whatever purpose, displayed in a market fair or any form of exhibit to the public. This test assists in preventing applications of varieties that are commonly known by the members of public or that have become common.

II. Distinct

365. Primarily a variety must contain characteristics that are distinct or different from the existing varieties. Under the Kenyan PVP law the plant variety must be sufficiently distinguishable by one or more important morphological, physiological or other characteristics from any other variety whose existence is a matter of common knowledge at the time of the application, whatever may have been the origin, artificial or natural, of the initial variation from which it resulted.

366. This test ensures that applicants do not apply and obtain exclusive rights over varieties that are or that have common characteristics and that are known to all save that they are not protected.

212. The Seeds and Varieties Act (1972), s. 2 of the Part II of the Fourth Schedule.
213. The Seeds and Varieties Act (1972), s. 2(a) of the Part II of the Fourth Schedule; In the case of trees or vines, this period extends to six years.

III. Uniform

367. The variety must be sufficiently uniform or homogenous having regard to the particular features of its sexual reproduction or vegetative propagation;

368. The distinct characteristics of the new variety must be capable of being uniform if produced under the same conditions as those proposed by the applicant. This ensures uniformity in the produce once farmed. This test also informs the benefits of the variety in the market. For instance if the applicant declares that the new variety is capable of producing or reproduction despite harsh climatic conditions, then such variety should ideally produce such high yields at all times when it is cultivated in harsh climatic conditions. It is however possible for a variety to show variations when cultivated as declared by the applicant. In such cases, the variance should not be so significant as to change the distinctive characteristics. It is accepted that there can be differentiated characteristics, but this difference should be marginal.

IV. Stable

369. The variety must be stable in its essential characteristics, that is to say, it may remain true to its description after repeated reproduction or propagation or, where the application prescribes a particular cycle of reproduction or multiplication, at the end of each cycle.

370. The variety's characteristics must remain unchanged throughout the propagation period. A variety must be capable of being described using identified characteristics that remain unchanged even when a variety is cultivated severally.

371. The test is often initialised as the (N) DUS test. These conditions form the test that the application for PVP is subjected to before a grant is issued. The test cannot be severed and is applied in whole thus a variety must pass the test before the grant can be issued. The test is applied by the government examiners who confirm whether or not a variety should be protected.

§4. Formalities (Procedure for Grant and Obtaining Protection)

372. An application for registration of PVP is addressed to the Managing Director, KEPHIS whose office is established under the KEPHIS Act (2012). In submitting the application, the applicant must also disclose the proposed name of the variety to which the application relates.[214] The proposed name is required:

- not to be similar to that of a plant variety of the same class as the variety in respect of which the application is made;

214. Seeds and Plant Varieties (Plant Breeders' Rights Regulations (1994), regulation 21.

- not nearly resemble the name of any other variety so as to be likely to deceive or cause confusion as to the identity of the variety;
- not to be likely to deceive or cause confusion as to the characteristics or value of the plant variety or as to the identity of the breeder;
- to conform with international usage as regarding the nomenclature of cultivated plants;
- not to be similar to or likely to be confused with a registered trade mark; trade name used in respect of the reproductive material of any kind; products of the plant variety in respect of which the application is made; or, products of a plant variety of the same class as the variety in respect of which the application is made; and
- to be desirable, in the opinion of the authorised officer.

373. Besides disclosing the proposed name, the applicant must also disclose the species or group of plant varieties to which the variety belongs; country in which the variety was bred or discovered; name of the breeder or discoverer; and whether the material from the variety has been offered for sale prior to the making of the application.[215]

374. Additionally, the applicant must fill a technical questionnaire, in which the following must be disclosed:

- the botanical and common names of the variety;
- proposed denomination (if available) and breeder's reference;
- information on the breeding scheme (whether the variety results from crossing, mutation, discovery or other method) and propagation of the variety (whether it is vegetatively propagated; propagated from seeds or in other manner);
- characteristics of the variety and their state of expression;
- similar varieties and the differences between these varieties and the applicant variety;
- any special conditions for growing the variety that may be required;
- whether the variety requires prior authorisation for release;
- information on plant material to be examined or submitted for examination; and
- whether the expression of a characteristic or several characteristics of a variety may be affected by factors, such as pests and disease, chemical treatment (e.g., growth retardants or pesticides), effects of tissue culture, different rootstocks, scions taken from different growth phases of a tree, etc.

375. The plant material should not have undergone any treatment which would affect the expression of the characteristics of the variety, unless the competent authorities allow or request such treatment. If the plant material has undergone such treatment, full details of the treatment must be given.

215. *Ibid.*

§5. Ownership and Transfer (Assignment: Licenses)

376. Section 23 of the Seeds and Plant Varieties Act (1972) deals with licensing of PVP. Subsection (1) gives the holder of the rights the power to grant any licenses that are necessary to stock the market with propagating material generated from plant breeding. The plant breeder will be required to furnish the licensee with the propagating material at a reasonable price if s/he is to make proper use of the license.[216]

377. Under the Act, compulsory licenses are granted by the Cabinet Secretary responsible for agriculture. Any person may apply for a compulsory license. The application may be granted if the Cabinet Secretary is of the opinion that the propagating material is not adequately stocking the market. Once so satisfied, the Cabinet Secretary will communicate with the holder of the PVP stating the reasons for his/her opinion and allow the proprietor to remedy the situation. If the PVP holder fails to do so, then the Cabinet Secretary will grant compulsory licenses to interested parties.[217] While settling the terms of compulsory licenses, the Cabinet Secretary is required to ensure that the plant variety subject to the license is available to the public at reasonable prices and that the PVP holder is reasonably remunerated.

378. Before granting a compulsory license, the Cabinet Secretary must be satisfied that the applicant is financially and otherwise in a position, and intends to, exploit the rights to be conferred in a business-like and competent manner and will not compromise the maintenance of the reproductive material concerned.[218] The Cabinet Secretary may also limit, extend, vary or revoke a compulsory license upon application by any party concerned.

379. When granting a compulsory license, it is immaterial whether or not the holder of the PVP has previously granted licenses to the applicant for a compulsory license or any other persons. Such compulsory license shall not be deemed to be an exclusive license. Any agreement purporting to bind a party not to apply for a compulsory license shall be void[219] as per section 23(12) of the Act.

§6. Scope of Exclusive Rights

380. Once granted PVP the rights holder is entitled to a bundle of rights which are controlled by the law. According to section 20 of the Seeds and Plant Varieties (Amendment) Act, 2012 the holder of PVP shall have the exclusive right to either by himself or through persons acting on his behalf to:

– produce or reproduce the variety;

216. Section 23(2), *Seeds and Plant Varieties Act*, Cap. 326, Laws of Kenya.
217. *Ibid.*, s. 23(3).
218. *Ibid.*, s. 23(8).
219. *Ibid.*, s. 23(12).

- condition the use of the variety for purposes of propagation;
- offer the variety for sale;
- sell or offer the variety for marketing;
- import the variety; and
- stock or reproduce the variety for any of the purpose set out above.

381. The rights holder is entitled to institute infringement proceedings against any person who does any of the above actions without his authority. This right is inclusive of the right to recover damages, obtain injunction, accounts of profits and any other remedy available in law for infringement.

382. The rights holder however has an obligation to ensure that the market is stocked with the protected propagating material and at reasonable process.[220] Where this is not possible, the rights holder is allowed to license third parties who are in a position to stock the market and at reasonable costs, terms and conditions.[221] In cases where the rights holder licenses third parties to market or sell on his behalf, he is still under an obligation to furnish the licensee with the protected propagating material he needs at a reasonable price if he is to make use of the license.[222]

§7. Limitations of the Scope of Protection

383. During the twenty-year period of protection, these rights are not deemed as infringed when the propagating material is produced or stocked for research purposes or for developing other new varieties.[223] This exemption assists other breeders to develop other varieties based on the existing and protected varieties. In cases where a farmer buys the propagated material, plants and saves the harvest and uses it in the next season such actions are not considered as infringement of the rights holder. Section 20 1E of the Seeds and Plant Varieties (Amendment Act (2012), recognises the need to balance the interests of the breeder with those of the farmers. It thus expressly allows a farmer to use the product of the harvest which they have obtained by planting, on their own holdings, the protected variety.[224] This flexibility allows farmers to save seed from their harvest for their next season. Inevitably, the farmers exchange such saved seeds between themselves with the aim of achieving the best out of their varieties.[225]

---

220. *Ibid.*, s. 23.
221. *Ibid.*
222. Seeds and Plant Varieties (Amendment) Act (2012), s. 23(2).
223. *Ibid.*, s. 20.
224. In ordinary cases, these actions would amount to infringement of right to the exclusive use to the variety. In the case of *Monsanto Canada Inc. v. Schmeiser* [2004] 1 S.C.R. 902, 2004 SCC 34 such use by the famer was held to be infringement and the Plaintiff could recover damages from the farmer.
225. In Kenya it is common for farmers to save and exchange seeds saved from previous harvest regardless of whether the plated material was protected by PVP or not.

§8. Duration of Protection

384. The above-mentioned rights are not absolute but are limited. An important limitation is in terms of the period of time that they are to be enjoyed. Kenya's PVP law provides that the rights holder shall enjoy the above rights exclusively for a continuous period of twenty years.[226] Tree and vines, however, enjoy a longer duration of protection for a period of twenty-five years.[227] Upon the expiry of the above period the propagating material falls into the public domain. The rights holder may however surrender some or all of the above rights as he may wish. These rights being property rights can be compulsorily acquired by the government.[228]

§9. Infringement and Remedies

385. PVP being private rights the rights holder has to institute proceedings to enforce them. Civil action on infringement may be brought under the Seeds and Plant Varieties Act (Cap. 326) and the Seeds and Plant Varieties (Amendment) Act, 2012. Herein, infringement cases are determined on a balance of probability and therefore dependent on the facts presented by the parties. The following key remedies are available in infringement cases: Injunctions, damages, and account of profits.

386. Under the Anti-Counterfeit Act, 2008 criminal action may also be taken against an infringer of PVP if a counterfeiting complaint is laid either before the Executive Director of the Anti-Counterfeit Authority or the Commissioner of Customs of the Kenya Revenue Authority depending on whether the infringing material is either in the country or at the border, respectively.

226. Seeds and Plant Varieties (Amendment) Act (2012), s. 19.
227. *Ibid.*
228. Seeds and Plant Varieties (Amendment) Act (2012), s. 23; any person can apply to the minister for the time being to compulsorily acquire a protected propagating material where the right holder does not satisfy the obligation of stocking or ensuring that the market is stocked.

Chapter 8. Chip Protection

387. In Kenya there is currently no law specifically providing for the protection of integrated circuit designs and integrated circuit masks.[229] A draft bill was prepared in the early 2000s but was not adopted by Parliament. Drawings of integrated circuit designs could possibly obtain protection under copyright law and/or industrial design law, although the functional nature of such drawings would call into question the suitability of such laws for the purpose. An analogy can be found in architectural works (buildings and models thereof), which are clearly functional and yet are specifically mentioned in the Copyright Act 2001 as receiving copyright protection.[230] There is no such specific mention in the Copyright Act for integrated circuits.

388. Provided that the relevant legal requirements (i.e., novelty, inventive step, usefulness) are met, integrated circuit layouts would find protection under the Kenyan patent and utility model laws. Indeed, the IPA 2001 provides a definition of Utility Model as including 'any form, configuration or disposition of element of some … electrical and electronic circuitry … '.[231]

389. Notwithstanding the lack of dedicated legislation, Kenya is a party to the Agreement on TRIPS as well as the EAC Common Market Protocol, both of which provide for the protection of layout designs of integrated circuits. By the operation of Article 2(6) of the Constitution of Kenya 2010, these international agreements automatically form a part of Kenyan law,[232] and are therefore discussed below.

§1. Sources – Legislation

390. Article 35 of TRIPS provides, in relevant part:

> Members agree to provide protection to the layout-designs (topographies) of integrated circuits (referred to in this Agreement as 'layout-designs') in accordance with Articles 2 through 7 (other than paragraph 3 of Article 6), Article 12 and paragraph 3 of Article 16 of the Treaty on Intellectual Property in Respect of Integrated Circuits …

391. The 1989 Treaty on IP in Respect of Integrated Circuits (also known as the Washington Treaty or Integrated Property in respect of Integrated Circuits Treaty

229. AUTHOR'S NOTE: the following text is identical to the text in the CyberLaw book from the same encyclopaedia and written by the same author (Rutenberg).
230. Copyright Act, s. 2.
231. Industrial Property Act, s. 2.
232. Although the Constitution of Kenya 2010 states explicitly that any 'treaty or convention ratified by Kenya shall form part of the law of Kenya,' it is widely argued that enabling legislation is still a requirement for such international agreements to have effect in Kenya.

(IPIC Treaty)) was never officially ratified by enough countries to go into effect but was later given effect by its incorporation into TRIPS. The relevant parts of the IPIC Treaty are as follows:[233]

> Article 3(1) (a) Each Contracting Party shall have the obligation to secure, throughout its territory, intellectual property protection in respect of layout-designs (topographies) in accordance with this Treaty. It shall, in particular, secure adequate measures to ensure the prevention of acts considered unlawful under Article 6 and appropriate legal remedies where such acts have been committed.
>
> Article 4 Each Contracting Party shall be free to implement its obligations under this Treaty through a special law on layout-designs (topographies) or its law on copyright, patents, utility models, industrial designs, unfair competition or any other law or a combination of any of those laws.

392. As per Article 4 of the IPIC Treaty, Kenya appears to have fully implemented its obligation under TRIPS with respect to the protection of integrated circuit designs by providing for such protection with (at least) UMCs.

393. In the EAC, Article 43 of the Common Market Protocol provides a mandate for Kenya and other member nations to work together in offering protection of integrated circuit designs. The relevant parts of the Protocol are as follows:

1. The Partner States undertake to cooperate in the field of intellectual property rights to:
   (a) promote and protect creativity and innovation for economic, technological, social and cultural development in the Community; and
   (b) enhance the protection of intellectual property rights.
2. For the purposes of paragraph 1, the Partner States undertake to cooperate in the [area of] layout designs of integrated circuits ...

§2. Subject Matter of Protection

394. Not applicable in this jurisdiction, but *see* Chapter 3.

§3. Conditions of Protection

395. Not applicable in this jurisdiction, but *see* Chapter 3.

§4. Formalities Procedure for Grant and Obtaining Protection

396. Not applicable in this jurisdiction, but *see* Chapter 3.

---

233. Treaty on Intellectual Property in Respect of Integrated Circuits, Arts 3–4.

§5. Ownership and Transfer (Assignment – Licenses)

397. Not applicable in this jurisdiction, but *see* Chapter 3.

§6. Scope of Exclusive Rights

398. Not applicable in this jurisdiction, but *see* Chapter 3.

§7. Limitations of the Scope of Protection

399. Not applicable in this jurisdiction, but *see* Chapter 3.

§8. Duration of Protection

400. Not applicable in this jurisdiction, but *see* Chapter 3.

§9. Infringement and Remedies

401. Not applicable in this jurisdiction, but *see* Chapter 3.

§10. Overlapping and Relation to Other Intellectual Property Laws

402. Not applicable in this jurisdiction, but *see* Chapter 3.

Chapter 9. Trade Secrets/Confidential Information

§1. Sources – Legislation

403. Broadly speaking, a trade secret refers to information held by an entity, typically a company, that satisfies two criteria: (1) access to the information is limited and restricted, and is therefore known to a finite group of persons; and (2) the information is commercially valuable precisely because it is restricted and known to a finite group of persons.

404. It should be stressed, however, that no trade secret law is currently present in Kenya, nor have there been any serious efforts to enact such a law. Accordingly, the information in this section is generalised from countries that do have trade secret protection and is provided for the sake of completeness in discussing various forms of IP.

§2. The protection of Trade Secrets/Confidential Information

I. Requirements of a Trade Secret

405. A trade secret is information that is intended to remain secret and is therefore known only to a finite group of persons. Furthermore, the entity holding the trade secret must put into place procedures and infrastructure that clearly shows the entity's desire to maintain the information as secret. Examples of such procedures and infrastructure include any or all of the following: marking documents as confidential; storing confidential documents in a secure location; enabling password protection, encryption, and other safety measures for all systems and electronic documentation containing or pertaining to the information; ensuring that all persons with access to the knowledge execute a non-disclosure agreement; and limiting access by third parties to production or other relevant facilities. This is not, of course, an exhaustive list, and trade secret lawsuits may involve judicial determination as to whether an entity made sufficient effort to maintain the secrecy of information.

406. The information may be known to a finite group of people, although the size of the finite group is not important. The information can be known to a large number of persons provided that those persons are sufficiently controlled, such as with the example measures mentioned above.

407. In order for information to qualify for trade secret protection, and in addition to the actions taken by the owner of the information to keep such information secret, it must often also be the case that the information is valuable to the owner on account of its secrecy. In other words, because of the secret information, and as long as the information remains secret, the owner derives added value. Such value can be intrinsic or can be derived from a competitive advantage that the information bestows to the owner. These are described below.

408. Examples of information with an intrinsic value include formulations and methods that allow a company to make a specific and unique product. The formulation of Coca-Cola, being known to a very limited number of people and having been kept a secret for over 100 years, is the quintessential example of this type of trade secret. The formulation for the mouthwash Listerine® and the recipe for chicken sold by KFC® are other examples.

409. Examples of information bestowing a competitive advantage generally fall into two categories. In the first category, the information allows a company to make a common product in a manner that is superior to competitors. Superiority can be obtained by making the same product at a lower cost and/or by producing a product of superior quality. In the second category, the information improves the competitive position of the company at any point in the production and sales process. In this category are lists of preferred customers and preferred suppliers, as generation of such lists often requires significant effort over a substantial period of time (including much trial and error). Competitor companies can clearly independently derive lists of preferred customers and suppliers, but when such information is accidentally or intentionally released to a competitor it represents a significant loss of competitive advantage for the original owner of the lists.

II. Effect of a Trade Secret

410. Employees that are privy to a trade secret are typically bound by a non-disclosure agreement, and may further be bound by a non-compete agreement. The latter stipulates that, if the employee leaves the employer for any reason, that employee is barred from starting a competing company and barred from becoming an employee of a competing company. Such agreements may be geographically limited and/or limited in time (e.g., valid for any competing company within the same physical market and/or valid for a period of five years). Some jurisdictions partially or completely prohibit such agreements as illegitimately limiting an individual's fundamental freedoms (e.g., freedom to contract, freedom of employment). California is the most significant example of such a jurisdiction, and the legal limitations on non-compete agreements in California are often cited as a factor that contributed to the success of Silicon Valley.

411. A valid trade secret can become known to an independent entity (e.g., a company not affiliated with the original owner of the secret) in a variety of ways, some of which are being legal and some of which being contrary to trade secret law. Independent development and reverse engineering are typical legal routes by which a trade secret can become known to an independent entity. Independent development is simply where a third party independently derives the information, without having access to the original trade secret or to any individuals with knowledge of the trade secret. Reverse engineering occurs, for example, when a third party obtains a product and determines how to make the same or similar product (e.g., by taking apart the product to determine the constituent components and deriving manufacturing techniques for such components). Trade secret laws generally do not prohibit reverse engineering, so product sales contracts frequently involve provisions against such behaviour.

412. Illegal means by which a trade secret can become known to a competitor third party include disclosure by a current or former employee, and industrial espionage, the latter often being regulated by criminal law. Disclosure by a current or former employee includes accidental disclosures as well as intentional disclosures. Liability for the damage resulting from improper disclosure rests with the employee or former employee, and may also rest with the receiving company if the receiving company knows that it is receiving confidential information.

III. Conclusions

413. Protection of IP via trade secrets is, in many respects, the exact opposite of protection via patents. As mentioned above, the purpose of patents is to widely disseminate technological advancements, and so the patent application is published after eighteen months of confidentiality. In return, a limited period of monopolistic style protection is offered to the patent applicant. Reverse engineering and independent development are not defences towards patent protection. In contrast, a trade secret law is designed to encourage tight control over technological advancements, and under ideal conditions the technology can remain secret essentially indefinitely. Reverse engineering and independent development by third parties are, however, allowed and encouraged under trade secret laws.

414. In Kenya, as mentioned, there is no specific law for the protection of trade secrets. Nevertheless, businesses in Kenya can sometimes rely on corporate, business, and contract laws to prevent the spread of secret technologies. For example, non-disclosure agreements and non-compete clauses are generally allowable in Kenya and can have similar effects to trade secret laws. Corporate espionage and other means of obtaining information can be actionable (or even criminal), particularly where such activities result in unfair advantages in a field of business.

Chapter 10. Geographical Indications and Appellations of Origin

§1. Introduction

415. 'Champagne,' 'Porto,' and 'Darjeeling' are examples of products whose names are known throughout the world and are associated with a certain nature or quality. It is important to note that these names have a geographical connotation designating existing places, towns regions or countries.[234] Due to the fact that they a great reputation, they are subject to misappropriation and counterfeiting by third parties who want to take advantage of the reputation to sell their products. For instance the use of the word 'Darjeeling' for the tea grown in Kenya even if the quality is the same or better than the tea from Darjeeling in India. One would buy the tea assuming that it is one or the same as the one from India. The geographical area has certain attributes that contribute to the product. Thus, even if one makes sparkling wine from Naivasha in Kenya, it cannot be called Champagne.

416. Geographical indications (GIs) are an area of IP, which have not been given as much attention as other areas of IP until recently. A GI is a sign used on products that have a specific geographical origin and possesses qualities or reputation that are due to that origin.[235] Unlike most IP, there are various concepts of protection under GIs, and the term only appeared recently in international negotiations. A GI may be defined as a legally protected sign or domination linking a product to a particular location, region or country. This right basically protects the goodwill associated with the name or advantages or characteristics that contribute to the reputation of quality of the product.[236] The legal definitions vary from one country to another and the Paris Convention does not contain the notion of a GI. However, there are two notions that are defined namely the indications of source and appellations of origin.[237]

417. An 'indication of source' means an expression or sign used to indicate that a product or a service originates in a country, region or specific place. Examples are labels saying 'Made in Kenya,' 'Product of South Africa' or 'Swiss Made.' An appellation of origin means a geographical name of a country, region or specific place which serves to designate a product originating therein the characteristic qualities of which are due exclusively or essentially to the geographical environment, including natural or human factors or both natural and human factors.[238] Examples include 'Champagne', 'Habana', 'Cognac' and 'Chianti' among others. Under the indications of source, no particular quality of the product if legally required and generally, the use of false or deceptive indications of source is illegal.

234. WIPO *WIPO Intellectual Property Handbook: Policy Law and Use* p. 120.
235. WIPO *Geographical Indications an Introduction* Publication 952 available online at www.wipo.int.
236. Abbot F et al. (1999) *The International Intellectual Property System: Commentary and Materials*, Hague, Kluwer International p. 185.
237. Article 1(2) of the Paris Agreement.
238. Abbot F et al. (1999) *The International Intellectual Property System: Commentary and Materials*, Hague, Kluwer International p. 185.

The appellations of origin on the other hand have specific attributes due exclusively or essentially to the geographical area, which contribute to the quality or desirable attributes of the product. The use of an appellation is restricted to a specific group of people located in a particular geographical area and only in connection with specific products. It is notable that the qualities are attributes to factors such as climate, soil, or traditional methods of production. Indications of source and appellations of origin provide protection against the deceptive use of local and geographical names in connection with a product unrelated to the region.[239]

418. According to Abott et al., GIs traditionally fulfil two main functions, namely:[240]

- to promote products with certain characteristics which are of considerable benefit to the region where the products originate or manufactured and the market for the products. GIs offer protection to the producers against unauthorised exploitation; and
- the GIs offer the consumer information as to the source of the product especially with an increasingly diversified market and they can make informed choices. The quest for specialised products generates demand for products with identifiable geographical origin.

419. A GI is 'a term that is often used broadly to embrace all forms of protection for indications of geographical origin, including both the indications of source and appellations of origin but is also given a more specific meaning in which case it usually implies something more than a mere indication of source but not necessarily meeting the full requirements of an appellation of origin, and it applies only to goods'.[241]

420. The concept of GIs originated in Europe and was mainly used for agricultural products and foodstuffs but has eventually evolved to include other industrial products. GIs have developed differently in different jurisdictions with different systems of protection. In some countries like the US, GIs are protected under Trademarks, while others have their own specific legal instrument. Due to increase in trade of GI products in international trade, there is a concerted move to harmonise the international regime.

---

239. Abbot F et al. (1999) *The International Intellectual Property System: Commentary and Materials*, Hague, Kluwer International p. 185.
240. *Ibid.*
241. O'Connor B. (2004) *The Law of Geographical Indications*, London, CMP Publishing Ltd., p. 23.

§2. PROTECTION OF GIS AT INTERNATIONAL LEVEL

421. As stated above, the protection of GIs was mainly done at the national level but with time it became necessary to have a harmonised system at international level. There are several international instruments that have tried to address this issue as will be discussed below.

I. The 1883 Paris Convention for Protection of Industrial Property

422. The Paris Convention was the first step towards international protection of GIs. The general principle of national treatment applies in the protection of industrial property including GIs.[242] Article 1(2) provides that: 'The protection of industrial property has as its object patents, utility models, industrial designs, trademarks, service marks, trade names, indications of source of appellations of origin, and repression of unfair competition.'

423. The protection covers indications of source and appellations of origin.

424. How do trademarks as discussed hereinabove differ from GIs? The Convention clearly draws a distinction between trademarks and GIs even though it does not define the term GIs. A trademark as discussed in the previous chapter is a sign or symbol or a combination thereof, which is used to distinguish the goods or services of one party from another. A GI on the other hand is not limited to a single producer but covers any number of producers who qualify for protection.

425. Article 9 establishes the principle of seizure upon importation must be provided for in cases of use of a false identification of source. As to who may request seizure on importation or the imposition of sanctions, the Convention states that it is the public prosecutor, any other competent authority, any interested manufacturer, or merchant, whether a natural person or legal entity engaged in the production, manufacture or trade in such goods.[243]

426. Article 10(1) is the basic provision under the convention on indications of source. It provides that the remedies in respect to Article 9 for unlawful use of trademarks or trade names shall apply to any use of false indication of source of a product. For the provision to be applicable, there is no need for the false indication to be physically present on the product. This is because any direct or indirect use including advertising will be actionable.[244] However, Article 10(1) will not apply in cases where the use of the name may be misleading but not false. For instance, if there

242. Article 2 of the Paris Convention.
243. Articles 9(3) and 10(2).
244. *WIPO Intellectual Property Handbook: Policy Law and Use* Publication 952 available online at www.wipo.int., (WIPO IP book) pp. 124–125.

are two areas, which have similar geographical conditions but are in different countries, the use of the indication of source, though misleading may not be actionable even where only one of the areas if known internationally.

427. Issues of unfair competition are addressed under Article 10*bis* as it provides protection against unfair competition as well as a basis for protection against use of confusing, false or misleading GIs. Member States are obliged under Article 10*bis* to provide protection against unfair competition, set a general definition of what constitutes unfair competition and contains non-exhaustive list of what types of acts that must be prohibited.[245] The following acts are prohibited under Article 10*bis:*[246]

- All acts which may create confusion, by any means with the establishment, the goods or the industrial or commercial activities of a competitor.
- False allegations in the course of trade of such nature that would discredit the establishment, the goods or the industrial or commercial activities of the competitor.
- Indications or allegations the use of which in the course of business is liable to mislead the public as to the nature, the manufacturing process, the characteristics, the suitability for their purpose or the quantity of the goods.

428. Associations and federations representing interested manufacturers, producers or traders may take action under certain conditions with the aim of curtailing false indications of source.[247] Article 10 does not make specific reference to appellations of origin but the use of the term 'indication of source' may be extended to cover protection of appellations of origin because they both receive the same treatment under the Convention and 'appellation of origin' may constitute at minimum an indication of source.[248]

429. Protection afforded by the Paris Convention covers a larger territorial space for Members of the Paris Union. The convention does not address the issue of indications, which are generic in some of the Member States but protected in another. Each Member State has the freedom to deal with it as they deem fit. The Convention does not provide special remedies against the infringement under Article 10*bis*.

II. The 1891 Madrid Agreement on Indications of Source

430. The Madrid Agreement for the Repression of False or Deceptive Indications of Goods is a special agreement within the Paris Union Framework and also covers repression of deceptive indications of source. This was the first agreement to

245. *Ibid.*
246. *Supra* note 241 pp. 29–30 (O'Connor B (2004) *The Law of Geographical Indications* London, CMP publishing Ltd).
247. Article 10*ter* Paris Convention.
248. For further reading *see* WIPO (1997) *Introduction to Intellectual Property: Theory and Practice* Kluwer International.

provide specific rules for the repression of false and deceptive indications of source. Although it does not add much to the protection offered under the Paris Convention, it extends protection to deceptive indications of source in addition to false indications.

431. Article 1(1) of the Madrid Agreement provides:

> All goods bearing a false or deceptive indication by which one of the countries to which the Agreement applies, or a place situated therein, is directly or indirectly indicated as being a country or a place of origin shall be seized on importation into any of the said countries.

432. Seizure shall be done upon importation into any of the States Party to the Madrid Agreement. The mode/procedure of seizure is also covered. Member States have the liberty to make provisions allowing private individuals to act after applying through the public prosecutor or any other competent authority.

433. Generic appellations are not protected and courts are given competence within the Member States to determine which indications fall outside the provisions of the Agreement because of their generic nature. This clearly stated in Article 4. National courts have often differed in their approach. However, only regional appellations concerning the source of products of the vine are excluded from the reservation inherent in the provision as it limits the scope of the Madrid Agreement.[249]

434. The ratification/accession of the Agreement is limited making it less effective and this may be attributed to various factors including the principle of registration based on home rules and inability of States to deal with the problem of names that may be considered generic or homonymous.

III. The Lisbon Agreement for the Protection of Appellations of Origin and Their International Registration

435. The Lisbon Agreement for the Protection of Appellations of Origin and their International Registration was adopted within the framework of Article 19 of the Paris Convention. The main principle under the Lisbon Agreement is that States Party to the Agreement shall undertake to protect the appellations of origin that are protected as such in the country of origin and registered in the international register under WIPO.[250]

436. Article 2(1) defines an appellation of origin as 'the geographical name of a country, region or locality, which serves to designate a product originating therein, the quality and characteristics of which are due exclusively or essentially to the geographic environment, including the natural and human factors'. Thus only names

249. *WIPO Intellectual Property Handbook: Policy Law and Use,* pp 124-125
250. Article 1(2) of the Lisbon Agreement.

that conform to this definition may be protected under the Agreement. From the definition, it is clear that for protection to be available, the appellation must be a geographical name of a country, region or locality. It must serve to designate a product originating in the country, region or locality in reference, and there must be a qualitative link between the product and the geographical areas. If the qualitative link is not sufficient, the name is not an appellation of origin but merely an indication of source.

437. The definition of the appellation of origin in the above article has as serious drawback for countries, which do not cover agricultural and handicraft products but only cover products of industry. Without the qualitative link between the product and geographical environment, even where human factors are sufficient, it is not possible to have the appellation of origin. It may be difficult to prove the link.

438. The definition of appellation of origin was extended to 'any usurpation or limitation, even if the true origin of the product is indicated or if the appellation is used in the translated form or accompanied by terms such as "kind," "type," "make," "imitation" or the like'.[251]

439. In order to be protected under the Lisbon Agreement, the appellation of origin must be recognised and protected as such in the country of origin and that the appellation of origin must be registered with the International Bureau of WIPO.[252] The protection granted by international registration under the Agreement is unlimited in time.

IV. The Stresa Convention of 1951

440. The International Convention on the Use of Appellations of Origin and Denominations of Cheese (Stresa Convention) was signed. This Convention applies mainly to cheese and came into force in September 1953. The Member States committed to prohibiting the use of false designations of origin on their territory and to ensure application of the Convention. It provided a higher level of protection for four GIs namely Gorgonzola, Parmagio Reggaiano, Pecorino Romano and Roquefort. The second level of protection was granted to other cheese namely Camembbert, Danablu, Edam, Emmental, Gruyère, Pinzgauer Berkäse or Somsö.

441. The Stresa Agreement was supplemented by the EU Regulation 2081/92 of 14 July 1992 and is thus no longer effective. It is interesting to note that although it was deemed to be an international convention, only four EU Member States were party to it.

251. Article 3 of the Lisbon Agreement.
252. Article 1.2.

V. Protection of GIs under TRIPS Agreement

442. Part II section 3 of the TRIPS Agreement covers protection of GIs and includes the definition and scope of GIs, minimum standards and common protection for all kinds of products, relationship between trademarks and indications of origin, additional protection for wines and spirits, negotiation and review of section III on GIs and exceptions to the protection. Article 22 defines GIs as 'Indications which identify a good as originating in the territory of a Member or a region or locality in that territory, where a given quality, reputation or other characteristic of the good is essentially attributable to its geographical origin.'

443. It expands the definition under the Lisbon Agreement and includes GIs, which do not necessarily have to be a geographical place. An example is the use of 'Basmati' for rice coming from India although it is not the name of a place as such. The goods to be protected should originate in the territory, region or locality to which it is associated.[253] The Agreement leaves it to the Member States to decide how to protect the GIs.

444. Article 22.3 governs the interrelationship between protection of trademarks and appellations of origin. More so in relation to registration of trademarks consisting of GIs. Wines and spirits are granted additional protection under Article 23.1. There are a number of exceptions and limitations contained in Article 24 of the Agreement. The first exception is the right of WTO Member States to allow continued and similar use of particular GI of another Member identifying wines and spirits.[254] The second exception relates to rights in trademarks.[255] The third relates to GIs of a Member State, which are considered by another Member State to be a term customary in common language as the common name for the goods or services.[256]

§3. Protection of GIs in Kenya

445. There is currently no specific legal instrument on protection of GI in Kenya. The Draft Geographical Bill has been pending for more than ten years. As a member of the WTO, Kenya is required to ensure that the minimum standards of protection as set out in the TRIPS Agreement are implemented. This section shall briefly look at the existing legal framework and how it can be used to protect GIs.

253. Blackeney M. 'Geographical Indications' in Blackeney M. et al. (eds) (2012) *Extending the Protection of Geographical Indications: Case Studies of Agricultural Products in Africa*, London Earthscan from Routledge p. 13.
254. Article 24.4 TRIPS Agreement.
255. Article 24.5 TRIPS Agreement.
256. Article 24.6 TRIPS Agreement.

I. Protection under the 2010 Constitution

446. The Constitution recognises IPR and obliges the State to ensure that adequate protection is granted for these rights. This is captured in Article 40.5, which requires the State to promote and protect IPR of the people of Kenya. Under Article 25, the general principles of international law shall form part of the law in Kenya.

II. Protection under Trademarks and Certification Marks

447. Generally, protection under Trademarks is limited as they may not qualify for trademark protection. Certification marks indicate that goods and services have specific qualities which may also cover the geographical origin. They denote certain qualities in the goods. The Trademarks Act defines Certification marks as:

> a mark adopted in relation to any goods to distinguish in the course trade goods or other characteristic from goods not so certified shall be registrable as a certification trademark in Part A of the register in respect of those goods in the name, as the proprietor thereof, of that person: Provided that a mark shall not be registrable in name of a person who carries on trade in goods of the kind certified.[257]

448. Producers who comply with the above standards may use the certification trademark and they have to ensure that the goods or services possess the certified quality. This makes it possible to use the trade certification marks for the protection of GIs in Kenya. Protection may also be done through the collective marks. A collective mark is defined as:

> A mark capable of distinguishing, in the course of trade, the goods or services of persons who are members of an association, from goods or services of persons who are not members of such an association, shall on application in the prescribed manner, be registrable as a collective mark in respect of the goods or services in the name of such an association.

449. Associations or cooperative societies may own the collective marks where they set the criteria for use of the marks. Example of collective marks in Kenya include Mwea Rice and Ahero Sugar.

III. The Draft GI Bill

450. The Draft GI Bill seeks to provide protection at national level in Kenya. The main features are the definition of GI, administration of GIs in Kenya and other relevant provisions as provided for in international treaties.

---

257. Section 40 of the Trademarks Act Cap. 506 of the laws of Kenya.

451. Kenya has not ratified/acceded to the Madrid Agreement or the Lisbon Agreement and for now has to rely on bilateral agreements to protect its GIs outside the country.

§4. SUMMARY AND CONCLUSION

452. There is a need to protect GIs in Kenya which will benefit various sectors of the society. For instance, branding of agricultural products that have a specific recognised quality such as 'Kericho Tea' will help move farmers from merely trading in raw materials to competitive trade at the global level as was the case with Ethiopian coffee. It is a well-known fact that due to the specific geographical conditions, Kenyan tea and Coffee have particularly sought after qualities and are used to blend with other products from other countries and this is a good case for GI protection.

453. Kenya should also try and pass the GI Bill which has been pending for too long yet occasioning lost opportunities for the country especially in areas where the potential GIs have been identified such as tea, Kitui Honey, Kisii Soapstone among others.

Chapter 11. Genetic Resources, TK and Traditional Cultural Expressions

§1. Introduction

454. Indigenous knowledge systems which encompass TK, traditional cultural expressions and use of genetic resources (GR) have been and continue to be an important aspect of local and indigenous communities all over the world. Indigenous and local communities had various systems such as customs and taboos that were used to protect, preserve and manage GR, TK and Traditional Cultural Expressions Policy's (TCEs). However, with the colonial era, these systems were relegated and replaced by laws and legal systems from the west, which did not take them into account.

455. However, with increased use of GR, TK and TCEs especially in the global market over the last twenty years, there was need to provide adequate protection of GR, TK and TCEs, provide for access and benefit sharing and prevent misuse and unlawful exploitation. This becomes more important where there is a presumption under the current IP system that since most of these knowledge systems are in the public domain. However, public domain is a construct of the IP system and to that extent may not be applicable in the case of GR, TK and TCEs even if they are considered common property. Commercial use of GR, TK and TCEs by third parties may also lead to misappropriation and misuse of the knowledge with may also deny the custodians the resulting benefits. There is thus a need to develop a system that allows for access and benefit sharing as well as ensuring protection and preservation of GR, TK and TCEs.

456. The increased significance of GR, TK and TCEs has led to more discussions in different areas, from food, agriculture, medicine, biological diversity, environmental issues, entertainment and other creative industries. This has brought about discussions on how to protect GR, TK and TCEs ether within the IP framework, other legal regimes or have its own system of protection. These are issues that have been and continue to be discussed at national, regional and international levels including within WIPO and ARIPO.

I. Rationale for Protection

457. It is important to note that among the indigenous and local communities, TK, GR and TCEs form part a holistic overview that is part and parcel of their being, customs, culture and way of life. There is a need to protect the works from unauthorised use or misuse, ensure access and benefit sharing as well as preservation. Most countries in Africa, including Kenya have rich cultural heritage, biological resources and the attendant TK. Indigenous and local communities hold this knowledge as part of their cultural identity.

458. There are many cases where important technology has been derived from TK without the consent of the custodians and commercially exploited without any benefit trickling down to them. This was well illustrated in the *Hoodia* case in Southern Africa. The San people of the Kalahari have over the years used the bitter flesh of the *Hoodia* plant to suppress hunger. In the 1960s, the Centre for Scientific and Industrial Research (CSIR) in South Africa developed an interest in the same and subsequently came up with P57, an anti-obesity/ appetite suppressant drug, for which it obtained a patent. CSIR later licensed the Phytopharm UK to invest and commercialise the drug. CSIR had signed an MOU with the representatives of the San People followed by a benefit sharing system. It is important to note that CSIR research was informed by existing TK of the San people which led to their research. In this case, CSIR recognised the San as the custodians of the TK as it related to the genetic resource.[258]

459. This case the *Hoodia* and others provide several reasons why we should protect GR, TK and TCEs. First is the increased interest in their use in trade, pharmaceuticals, agriculture and management of the environment. It is important to define the parameters for use within a proper policy, legal and institutional framework. Second is the issue of preservation of knowledge. For most communities in Africa, the knowledge was passed on orally from generation to generation until recently. One elder in the Maasai community once stated that once an elder dies in the community, they die with the knowledge. It sets out the need not only for protection but documentation of the same. Third, is the issue of unauthorised use and exploitation by third parties? A proper legal system will ensure that the knowledge is used with the consent of the custodians and used for the purposes for which it was intended. This in turn will ensure benefit sharing and at the same time allow for access.

II. Types of Protection

460. As stated above, protection would either be within the existing IP framework, which has its own limitations, use of other legal regimes or have a sui generis system of protection as has been developed at national and regional level. There are two types of protection that may be granted for protection namely:

(a) Defensive Protection ensures that third parties are stopped from acquiring rights over TK. There are different defensive strategies that may be employed such as creation of databases to provide information. This worked in the *Turmeric* case where the where the United States Patent and Trademark Office (USPTO) granted a patent which was later revoked for the use of *turmeric* to treat wounds. This was a property that was well known in India where it had been used for centuries and was well documented. It is important for countries in Africa to develop a database on GR, TCEs and TK as it relates to GR. This may also be

258. For more information on the case study, *see* http://www.wipo.int/export/sites/www/academy/en/about/global_network/educational_materials/cs1_hoodia.pdf.

used to protect sacred symbols and other TCEs especially against registration as trademarks. Creation of a TK commons is also a good strategy for defensive protection as it also ensures preservation of knowledge.

(b) Positive Protection provides for granting of rights to the custodians of GR, TK and TCEs to promote their knowledge, control its use including how it may or may not be used and ensure that they benefit from any commercial exploitation the knowledge. This type of protection is similar to what is granted under IP law and the rights may be exclusive collective rights. There are some laws that grant both defensive and positive protection like the ARIPO Swakopmund Protocol and the proposed TK Bill in Kenya.

461. Protection of GR, TK, and TCEs may be through the existing IP system such as patents, industrial designs, GIs, copyright and related rights and utility models. IP protection is inadequate for protection as they are incompatible and were not designed to protect the same due to various limitations as previously discussed. The most advisable way is to devise a sui generis legal regime that is specific to TK, GR, and TCEs and ensures that the knowledge is safeguarded, prior informed consent is obtained in the case of innovations and derivative works, provide for access and equitable/fair benefit sharing and also provides recognition of the custodians.

§2. Protection at Various Levels

I. Protection at International Level

462. Protection of TK, GR and traditional cultural expressions is yet to be developed especially as it relates to IP.

463. As stated in the introduction, the need to have an international regime for protection of GR, TK and TCEs has increased over the last thirty years. This may be attributed to several factors, which include the increased use of GR and TK in various sectors such as the pharmaceutical and cosmetics industries. There have been attempts to have protection of GR, TK, and TCEs within existing IP and other laws. The Convention on Biological Diversity (CBD) 1992 to a certain extent protects TK and GR and provides a legal framework for preservation as well as promoting exchange of information including indigenous knowledge and TK.[259] CBD has the potential of encouraging exchange of information especially for purposes of research and development.

464. Another instrument that addresses this protection is the ITPGRFA (International Seed Treaty) 2001 which, recognises the contribution of indigenous and local communities in agriculture, conservation and development of new plant varieties as well as benefit sharing. The International Union for the Protection of New Plan Varieties (UPOV) Convention provides a sui generis form of IP protection specifically for plant breeding, which encourages the development of new plant varieties. It is

259. Articles 1, 8(j) and 17 of the CBD.

important to note that through the use of TK in existing GR including agricultural plants may to c certain extent be protected under this Convention to the extent that it fulfils the requirements. The UN Declaration of Rights of Indigenous Peoples (2007) also provides for the rights of indigenous peoples in maintaining and strengthening their own institutions, culture and tradition. Convention for the Safeguarding of the Intangible Cultural Heritage (2003) also makes provisions for the protection and preservation of intangible cultural heritage.

465. In the area of IP, the PCT 1970 which provides for patent application filing may to a certain extent be used in the protection of GR and TK. This may be through the examination of patents filed using GR and TK for novelty, which is one of the requirements for patentability. In the case of TCEs, the Berne Convention

466. It is important to note that the existing IP system focuses on the traditional IP rights as this was fashioned during the age of industrialisation in the West.[260] The system does not fully protect GR, TK and TCEs as most fall outside the scope of protection. Many countries have called for a sui generis system of protection. The IP systems would have major limitations as there are certain categories or criteria that have to be fulfilled such as fixation, originality, criteria for patentability, ownership, term of protection and management of GR, TK and TCEs that are common to more than one community in different geographical areas. In 2000, WIPO Member States established the Intergovernmental Committee on IP and Genetic Resources, Traditional Knowledge and Folklore (IGC) to look into the possible protection of GR, TK and TCEs. In 2009, the Committee agreed to work towards the development of an international legal instrument(s) and the process is still on going. There are various issues such as definitions, beneficiaries, access and benefit sharing which need to be discussed and agreed upon.

II. Protection at Regional Level

467. There are several instruments that have been developed in different regions. There have been several attempts to have an instrument that deals with issues of access and benefit sharing at the continental level especially as it relates to biological resources. These can be traced back to the then Organisations of African Unity (the predecessor to the Africa Union), which adopted the African Model Legislation for the Protection of the Rights of Local Communities, Farmers and Breeders and the Regulation of Biological Resources. The model law recognises the rights of local communities over GR, TK, farmers' rights, local innovation and practices.[261]

---

260. WIPO Briefing Paper No. 2 'The WIPO Intergovernmental Committee on Intellectual Property and Genetic Resources, Traditional Knowledge and Folklore' http://www.wipo.int/export/sites/www/tk/en/resources/pdf/tk_brief2.pdf.

261. Regional Laws on Traditional Knowledge and access to genetic resources http://biocultural.iied.org/regional-laws-traditional-knowledge-and-access-genetic-resources.

468. The ARIPO held several consultations, meetings and negotiations among the Member States that resulted in the ARIPO Swakopmund Protocol in August 2010, Swakopmund, Namibia. The protocol only covers TK and TCEs and ARIPO has yet to develop an instrument for the protection of GR. The protocol provides definitions for TK and TCEs, provides for protection, makes provisions for access and benefit sharing, defines the beneficiaries, provides for exceptions and limitations and compulsory licensing. The Protocol provides a basis for ARIPO Member States to develop their laws on protection of TK, and TCEs; the Traditional Knowledge Act in Kenya is an example that has borrowed from the protocol.

§3. Genetic Resources

469. The CBD defines GR as parts of biological material that contain information of value, are capable of reproducing or being reproduced and include plant or animal material or material of microbial origin such as medicinal plants, agricultural crops and animal breeds. Protection of GRs as earlier discussed is covered under the CBD and its Nagoya Protocol and the International Treaty on Genetic Resources for Food and Agriculture. GR become of interest when they are used for various innovations that are subsequently subject to patent protection as was the case with *Hoodia* and *Turmeric.* In 2014, the County Government of Baringo signed an agreement with a Dutch company on commercial exploitation, access and benefit sharing for an enzyme found in Lake Bogoria. The enzyme is used in various industries including textile, and paper. These cases illustrate the importance of defensive protection of GR and associated TK.

470. Defensive protection systems such as the TK digital library is important in determining prior art and avoid granting patents for works that have been derived from GR and associated TK. It is possible for countries to enact legislation at national level that provides for the disclosure requirement that also relies on prior informed consent. This has yet to be agreed upon at international level. Other areas of discussion include fair and equitable benefit sharing.

§4. Traditional Knowledge

471. There are various definitions for TK and as stated before, these are issues that are yet to be decided at the international level. The Swakopmund Protocol provides that TK refers to:[262]

> any knowledge originating from a local of traditional community that is the result of intellectual activity and insight in a traditional context, including know-how, skills, innovations, practices and learning, where the knowledge is embodied in the traditional lifestyle of a community or contained in the codified knowledge systems passed on from one generation to another. The term

262. Article 2.1 Swakopmund Protocol.

shall not be limited to a specific technical field, and may include agricultural, environmental or any medical knowledge associated with genetic resources.

472. WIPO defines TK as a living body of knowledge passed on from generation to generation within a community. It often forms part of a people's cultural and spiritual identity. The main aspects of TK are that it is knowledge, found in a traditional context and is passed from generation to generation. Some TK is closely associated with GRs as was laid out in the *hoodia* case, through utilisation and conservation of the resource from one generation to another. The TK normally provides researchers with information that will eventually lead them to isolate the relevant compound within the GR. Holders or custodians of TK always stress the importance of the holistic relationship between their TK and GR which is proving to be quite significant in various sectors including medicine, agriculture and other industrial applications.

§5. Traditional Cultural Expressions

473. According to WIPO, TCEs otherwise known as expressions of folklore may include music, dance, art, designs, names, signs and symbols, performances, ceremonies, architectural forms, handicrafts and narratives, or many other artistic or cultural expressions. They are part of the identity or heritage of an indigenous or local community, an expression of their traditional culture and are passed on from one generation to another. The Swakopmund Protocol provides a more elaborate definition;

474. Expressions of folklore include any forms, whether tangible or intangible in which traditional culture and knowledge are expressed, appear or are manifested and comprise the following forms of expressions or combinations thereof:

(i) verbal expressions such as but not limited to stories, epics, legends, poetry, riddles and other narratives; words, signs, names and symbols;
(ii) musical expressions such as but not limited to songs and instrumental music;
(iii) expressions by movement, such as but not limited to dances, plays, rituals and other performances; whether or not reduced to a material form; and
(vi) tangible expressions, such as productions of art, in particular drawings, designs, paintings(including body painting), carvings, sculptures, pottery, terracotta, mosaic, woodwork, metal ware, jewellery, basketry, needlework, textiles, glassware, carpets, costumes; handicrafts, musical instruments and architectural forms.

475. Section 2 of the UNESCO-WIPO Model Provision considers expressions of folklore as 'productions consisting of characteristic elements of the artistic heritage developed and maintained by a community or a country or by individuals reflecting the traditional artistic expectations of such community.'

476. It is clear from the above definitions that these refer to the creative works that have been within a community for generations.

§6. TK Commons

477. TK commons may be defined as particular institutional forms of structuring rights to access, use and control of TK, traditional cultural expressions and GR. The concept of commons is derived from the idea of community ownership of property founded on the principle that certain resources and things both tangible and intangible are owned and shared by a community of people and guided by predetermined set of rules and regulations which set the boundaries and limitations of such use.[263] The TK commons offers a defensive protection in the protection and conservation of TK, TCEs and GRs as it places the responsibility on the community that holds the knowledge and gives them the power to control how it is used and at the same time ensuring access and none of the knowledge is lost.

§7. Protection of GR, TK and TCEs in Kenya

478. Kenya, like most countries in Africa has a rich cultural heritage, TK and has diverse GR. TK covers know-how skills and practices that have been passed on from generation to generation and includes traditional medicine, crop and animal husbandry, rituals and preservation of food, management and preservation of the environment and other GR. Traditional cultural expressions cover music, art and handicrafts, folktales and dances. We have had numerous cases of bio-prospecting based on existing TK as it relates to the use of GR.

479. A widely held belief remains that the *kikoy* and the *Kiondo* have been appropriated by third parties using IP but fortunately that is not true. However the case is true for the 'extremophile' enzyme that was extracted from an organism found in Lake Bogoria in the 1990s. A biotechnology firm Genencor International sold the enzyme to Procter & Gamble where Gamble ultimately used this enzyme to develop an extremely successful line of Tide bleach that was used to stonewash denim. The Kenya Wildlife service threatened to sue the company but never came round to it. However, in 2014, the Baringo County Government came to an agreement with a Dutch Company for a royalty payment.

480. This underscores the need for a proper legal framework on the management and use of GR and their associated TK. There is now a specific legal framework for protection of GR, TK and TCEs, as well as several related laws that may be used to provide some form of protection.

481. The Genetic Resources, TK and TCE of 2009 lays down the policy framework for protection of TK, GRs and TCEs in Kenya. The main objective of the

263. Nonini, D.M. (2007), *The Global Idea of the 'Commons'*, Berghahn Books, New York pp. 1–25.

policy is to enhance and coordinate the application of TK, innovations and practices, use of GR and sustainable development in Kenya. The policy and the Constitution form the basis of the proposed laws, which will be discussed at the end of this section.

I. The Constitution of Kenya

482. The Constitution of Kenya 2010, provides a strong basis for an effective legal framework in protection on TK, TCEs and GRs. Article 11(2) provides that the State shall promote all forms of cultural expressions, recognise the role of science and indigenous technologies in the development of the country. Article 11(3) provides

483. Parliament shall enact legislation to (a) ensure that communities receive compensation or royalties for the use of their culture and cultural heritage and (b) recognise and protect the ownership of indigenous seeds and plant varieties, their genetic and diverse characteristics and their use by communities in Kenya. In an attempt to meet the constitutional requirements, the TK Bill 2015 was published and is to be passed into law in 2016 within the constitutional deadline. The protection of GRs is still under discussion but is also to be finalised in 2016.

484. Article 44(1) provides that: every person has the right to participate in the cultural life of their choice. Article 69(1) requires the State to ensure sustainable exploitation, management and conservation of GR and the environment and ensure equitable benefit sharing, protect and enhance IP in and indigenous knowledge, of and biodiversity and GR of the communities and also ensure that environmental and natural resources are utilised for the benefit of the people of Kenya.

II. Traditional Knowledge Act 2016

485. Taking into account the limitations of IP protection and the provisions under the Constitution, the Protection of Traditional Knowledge and Traditional Cultural Expressions Act was passed in August 2016 as one of the Bills that had to be passed in conformity with the provisions of Article 11(3) of the Constitution. It was the result of a consultative process, which was spearheaded by the Task Force under the KECOBO. The Act borrows from the ARIPO Swakopmund Protocol on the protection of TK and Traditional Cultural Expressions.

A. Traditional Knowledge

486. Part II of the Act deals with protection of TK which is generated, preserved and transmitted from one generation to another but within a community for economic, ritual, narrative or recreational purposes. It also recognises that the knowledge may be generated individually or collectively and is an integral part of the cultural identity of the community to which is distinctly associated with. Protection is not subject to any formality, but the law provides for creation of registers/ registration of TK. This would mainly be for defensive purposes.

487. The rights granted to the TK holder include the right to authorise the exploitation of their TK and to prevent exploitation without prior informed consent. The owners have a right to take legal action against any third party who illegally exploits the rights. To ensure compliance, each community has the right to make and adopt rules of procedure for authorisation.

B. Traditional Cultural Expressions

488. Like TK, TCEs are recognised and protected by the Act. The protection covers cultural expressions in whatever form including products of cumulative intellectual activity which are characteristic of a community's cultural identity and heritage and have been developed and maintained, used or developed by a community in accordance with its customary laws and practices. TCEs should also be generated, preserved and passed from one generation to another within the community for economic, ritual, narrative, decorative and recreational purposes and these could be individually or collectively generated. They should be integral to the cultural identity of the community.

489. No formalities are required for protection to be granted, but the government is allowed to provide for registration and maintenance of registers of TCEs within the country and national and county level.

C. Administration and Enforcement

490. The Act provides for the administrative framework both at the national and county level, the need for prior informed consent and access and equitable benefit sharing. The national government is meant to consult with the county governments to prevent acts of misappropriation, misuse and unlawful access and exploitation of TK and TCEs. Users shall be required to obtain prior informed consent and the utilisation of the TK and TCEs shall be compatible with fair practice, relevant customary laws, protocols and existing practices. Written authorisation is required for the use of TK and TCEs.

III. Protection under Copyright

491. The Copyright Act gives a definition of expressions of folklore. However, TCEs do not fall within the categories of works that are eligible for copyright protection. However, section 28 provides for protection of sound recordings. This means that the sound recording embodying the expressions of folklore will enjoy protection as a related right. Fixed performances of expressions of folklore may also be protected as performances under section 29 of the Act. Section 49 gives the Attorney General the power to authorised the use of expressions of folklore by third parties for commercial purposes. The fees collected are to be used for promotion of cultural activities. However, use of the works for non-commercial purposes and by the government is permitted without seeking the authority.

IV. Protection under the IPA

492. The IPA provides for protection of patents, industrial designs and utility models. TK would not be eligible for patent protection per se as most would not meet the criteria for patentability or protection under utility models or industrial designs.

V. Trademarks Act

493. The Trademarks Act, may to a certain extent be used to protect TK and traditional cultural expressions in Kenya. This is because trademarks are used by one person to distinguish his goods or services from those of his competitor and they are a mark of quality. Protection under trademarks is indefinite as long as the registration is renewed. Local and indigenous communities that hold TK and traditional cultural expressions may use collective marks for protection and this would be in line with the age-old tradition of branding their goods and services. In a recent case, a UK firm would have succeeded in registering *Kikoy* as a trademark in the UK denying many local entrepreneurs the use in the UK.

VI. Environmental Management and Coordination Act and Regulations

494. These provide for access and benefit sharing.

A. *National Museums and Heritage Act*

495. The Act deals with identification, protection, conservation and transmission of cultural and natural heritage in Kenya. The Act may be used to protect TK as it relates to culture and heritage as well as traditional cultural expressions and to a certain extent, GR that are part of the tangible cultural heritage.

§8. Summary and Conclusion

496. Protection of GR, TK and TCEs may best be served through a sui generis system which specifically addresses the issues of control of use, access and benefit sharing, protection against misappropriation and misuse as well as ensuring their preservation. While national laws may offer protection within the country and prevent access, due to the increased global trade and exchange of information, it is important to have an international regime that provides the necessary protection across the borders. It is important that local and indigenous communities protect and benefit from the use of their GRs, TK and TCEs.

Chapter 12. Enforcement

§1. Introduction

497. Effective enforcement of IPR is important for a vibrant IP system necessary for social-economic growth. An effective enforcement regime ensures conformity to law, involves constant review of existing laws as well as the administrative/institutional structures. It also requires adoption of new procedures and technologies for greater compliance.

498. Prior to the TRIPS Agreement, enforcement was largely left to the Member States at national level. The procedures for enforcement varied from country to country as there was no minimum standard at international level. Article 9 of the Paris Convention (1967 Act) made provisions for Member States on seizure of imported goods, which had illegal trademarks. Under Article 6*bis* (1) and 6 *septies* (2) Member States may make provisions for injunctive relief for wrongful use of well-known marks. On copyright, the Berne Convention (1971 Act), Article 13(3) makes provisions for seizure of recordings imported without the author's or rights holder's authority. Article 16 allows Member States to seize infringing copies within their national legal framework. Lack of harmonisation of these laws led to problems in enforcement. For instance, before Uganda enacted its new copyright law in 2006, unauthorised commercial use of copyright works especially music was rampant in Uganda which was deemed to be a haven for piracy. This was because the old Copyright Act in Uganda did not criminalise these activities and the illegal products found their way into the Kenyan market to the detriment of the local industry.

499. The TRIPs Agreement changed this, as it required all the WTO Member States to ensure that they put in place effective enforcement procedures.

§2. International Frameworks

I. Enforcement under the TRIPS Agreement

500. Part III of the TRIPs Agreement is one of the most significant changes in the IP landscape as it provides for minimum standards of enforcement of IP at international level.

A. General Obligations

501. Article 41 of the Agreement makes general provisions where Member States are required to make provisions for fast, expeditious remedies in line with the Agreement for effective action on IP infringement without creating any barrier to trade. The remedies should be fair and equitable and uncomplicated and based on the tenets of natural justice. This provides the framework for harmonisation of enforcement at regional and international level. Taking into account existing judicial systems, TRIPS does not require creation of specialised courts to deal with IP infringement cases.

B. Civil and Administrative Procedures and Remedies

502. Civil and Administrative remedies play an important role in cases of infringement of IPR. Under Articles 41 to 48 of the Agreement, these procedures should be fair and equitable. Evidence shall be secured and made available to the courts through relevant legal procedures. Remedies to be made available by national laws include damages, injunctions and other remedies that may be deemed necessary to create and effective deterrent to infringement, such as delivery up and disposal of infringing goods through court orders. The provisions also cover right to information and indemnification of the defendant. Article 48 allows for administrative procedures may be employed within the legal framework in relation to any of the civil remedies.

C. Provisional Measures

503. Provisional measures are necessary to preserve evidence in cases of suspected infringement. Under Article 50, the laws may provide for courts to grant prompt and effective provisional measures in order to prevent infringement and to preserve evidence in relation to an alleged infringement. This forms the basis of the Anton Piller Order, which has been successfully used in various cases.

D. Special Requirements Relating to Border Measures

504. With increased world trade and cross-border trade, goods and services are continuously moving from one country to another requiring specific legal provisions to ensure that only legitimate goods and services cross the borders or are involved in regional and international trade. Articles 51 to 60 require Member States to make specific provision in relation to border measures. These provisions empower customs officials to suspend the release of suspected infringing imported goods (counterfeit and pirated goods) where there are valid grounds that the goods are infringing. This is subject to a process that has to be documented, security and indemnification provided, and relevant notices issued. Competent Authorities like the Anti-Counterfeit Agency (ACA) may be granted ex officio powers to deal with infringement. Remedies in relation to border measures include orders to destroy the infringing goods. Re-exportation of counterfeit goods is not permitted as this will subject the goods to a different customs procedure and will not remove them from channels of commerce. It is notable that although Article 60 States that *de minimis imports* may be excluded from the above provisions, many countries clearly make it illegal for one to import infringing items in their luggage even for personal use.

E. Criminal Procedures

505. As stated earlier, many countries did not criminalise infringement of IP and instead made provisions for civil remedies and administrative action. For instance, although the Trade Marks Act Cap. 506 of Kenya provides for infringement, it does not make provisions for criminal sanctions. Article 61 clearly states that the laws shall provide for criminal procedures in relation to counterfeit of trademarks and copyright piracy at a commercial scale. The remedies include both fines and custodial sentences or both depending on the gravity of the offence. Part V of the Agreement deals with dispute prevention and settlement.

II. WIPO Treaties and Enforcement

506. The Paris Convention and the Berne Convention as stated earlier hardly had any provision on enforcement of IPR. In 1996, the WIPO Copyright Treaties as discussed in Chapter 4 were adopted. Both the WPPT and the WCT require contracting parties to put in place effective and expeditious enforcement procedures that provide remedies to deter infringement of rights conferred under Berne, TRIPS and other instruments that deal with the 'digital agenda.' These provisions are also found in the Beijing Treaty on Audiovisual Performances and the Marrakesh Treaty to Facilitate Access to Published Works for Persons Who Are Blind, Visually Impaired, or Otherwise Print Disabled. Interestingly, the Trade Mark Law Treaty 1994 and the Singapore Treaty on the Law of Trade Marks 2006 do not cover enforcement as they mainly cover the administration of trademarks. WIPO currently has an ad hoc Advisory Committee on Enforcement established in 2002 by the General Assemblies and mandated to provide technical assistance and coordination in the field of enforcement and does not deal with norm setting activities.

507. The WIPO Arbitration and Mediation Centre offers alternative dispute resolution mechanisms. The arbitration offers a cheaper, faster and effective means of determining cases at international level. The arbitrators and mediators are more conversant/specialised in IP and are likely to provide a more informed decision.

§3. Enforcement of IP in Kenya

508. Enforcement of IP law in Kenya has been quite a challenge. Although there are specific laws and institutions that deal with enforcement, compliance with the law is not optimal. The Copyright Act Cap. 130 of the Laws of Kenya, the Anti-Counterfeit Act Cap. 130A, The Trademarks Act, Cap. 506 The IPA are the main legal instruments that deal with enforcement of IP. Other legislations include the Evidence Act, Criminal Procedure Code and Civil Procedure Act. The main institutions that deal with enforcement are the KECOBO, the ACA, the National Police Service, the Judiciary, and the Customs Department. Industry organisations and standards organisations such as the Kenya Bureau of Standard and the Weights and Measures Department also contribute to the enforcement of IPR.

I. Copyright and Related Rights

509. The Copyright Act contains provisions for enforcement in compliance with the TRIPs Agreement. These include administrative actions, provisional measures, criminal procedures and civil actions. As stated in Chapter 4, section 35 of the Act lays out the acts of infringement that give rise to civil action while section 38 provides for infringement that would lead to criminal sanctions. The main institutions charged with enforcement of copyright include the Judiciary, KECOBO, National Police, Customs and Industry Organisations

A. *Kenya Copyright Board*

510. The KECOBO is a state corporation established to administer and enforce copyright and related rights in Kenya. KECOBO has put in place various systems to ensure enforcement of copyright and related rights. The Board has a Legal department comprised of copyright inspectors from the enforcement unit and copyright prosecutors.

1. Anti-piracy Measures

511. Section 36 of the Act requires that all audio and audiovisual works have an anti-piracy security device, which is a tamper-proof sticker that can be used to differentiate the legitimate copyright works from the illegal works. This is only useful for the physical works, and there is a need to come up with a digital version for the same. It has been used mainly by rights holders in the music industry and to a certain extent has helped in reducing the level of piracy for the works on which the stickers are affixed. The uptake has been slow due to various factors including cost and changes in technology. Success of the anti-piracy security device depends on various factors such as cooperation from rights holders; it must be practical and not easily replicated in the market and be applied to all products. Quite a number of rights holders have not affixed it on their works making enforcement difficult.

512. To ensure that all legitimate works, section 36, makes it illegal for one to release works into channels of commerce without affixing the anti-piracy security device. In addition, section 36 also makes it illegal to copy and reproduce the anti-piracy security device without authority. This has helped in enforcement of copyright, as under the same section, one is liable to criminal prosecution with a fine not exceeding KES 2 million or a prison term not exceeding ten years or both. There have been arguments that section 36 contravenes Article 5(2) of the Berne Convention. However, it does not create a formality for enforcement of rights but instead allows for better enforcement. This may be equated to the provision in the US Copyright law that provides for statutory damages only in cases where one has registered their works with the Registrar of Copyright.

513. Collective management of rights especially in areas such as music, film and book publishing is essential as it reduces levels of piracy through provision of accessible licensing schemes for users. This also applies to use of works in the digital environment, where it might to be possible to reach the individual author/rights holder to get permission to access or use works.

514. Other anti-piracy measures include digital watermarks, technological protection measures such as encoding signals, copy protection measures and other mechanisms that may be used to deter reproduction and subsequent distribution of works especially within digital networks. Enforcement of rights has become a challenge in the era of ever-changing technology and high-speed Internet. Ease of reproduction and distribution and modes of delivery have made it difficult to enforce rights and thus need to come up with solutions to keep up with these changes. Section 35 makes it illegal for one to circumvent technological protection measures and remove rights management systems or sell or manufacture a device that may be used to commit the above acts.

2. Inspection, Seizure and Prosecution

515. KECOBO has copyright inspectors who are appointed under section 39 of Cap. 130. Copyright Inspectors, on receiving information or report of an alleged infringement, are required to carry out investigations. They have authority to enter premises that are suspected to have infringing works or being used to reproduce/manufacture infringing works and seize the items to be used as exhibits in subsequent court cases. Persons suspected to be infringing on copyright are arrested by copyright inspectors and arraigned in court. The law sets out specific procedures in relation to seizure of goods to ensure that they are well documented and preserved. Once goods have been seized and all documentation done, the matter is handed over to the prosecutors for necessary action.

3. The Competent Authority

516. The Competent Authority is an ad hoc tribunal established under section 48 of Cap. 130 to deal with disputes arising from administrative actions by KECOBO such as licensing of collective management organisations and disputes arising from the activities of collective management organisations.

4. Judiciary

517. The Judiciary determines both criminal and civil cases and also grants provisional orders such as the Anton Piller Orders.

a. Civil Actions

518. Any person who exercises the exclusive rights granted under the Copyright Act, without the authority of the rights holder will be liable to civil action. These unauthorised acts include reproduction, sale, distribution, rental and import of copyright-protected works. A third party will also be liable for infringement where they circumvent technological protection measures, manufacture or distribute devices that may be used to circumvent technological protection measures or removes or alters electronic rights management systems, imports, distributes or makes available to the public works where the electronic rights management systems have been removed. The rights holder has the following causes of action against the alleged infringer:

(i). Anton Piller Orders

519. The Anton Piller Order is one of the most effective methods that may be used to secure and preserve evidence in cases of suspected infringement prior to the court case. This is well captured in Article 50 of the TRIPs Agreement, which refers to preservation of evidence. Section 37 of Cap. 130 provides that a person may apply for Anton Piller Orders where there is prima facie evidence that his rights have been infringed, he has a cause of action against the person he seeks to pursue, that the other party has in his possession works that would form part of the evidence in the cause of action and that there is a real and well-founded apprehension that the infringing works may be destroyed, hidden or made inaccessible before the court action. The courts have to be sure that the procedure, which is a pre-emptive measure is not abused. In the case *Microsoft Corporation v. Mitsumi Computer Garage Ltd* [2001] 1 EA 127, court granted the applicants Anton Piller Orders ex parte, which allowed them to get into the respondents' premises to secure evidence that was used in the main suit. It is important to note that these orders are only applicable for a limited duration and will cease if the main suit does not materialise.

(ii). Injunctions

520. Under section 35(4)(i), courts may grant injunction on application by the rights holder. These may either be prohibitory or negative in nature, based on principles of equity. In copyright infringement cases, courts are more liberal in granting permanent or temporary injunctions due to the nature of copyright and the length of time taken to determine cases. If the injunctions are not granted, the rights holder stands to suffer irreparable damages as these works can easily be reproduced and distributed especially on digital networks. Interim injunctions grant temporary relief as they stop the infringement and also prevent future acts of violation of rights.

521. The principles on which courts grant injunction in Kenya are laid down in *Anielo Giella v. Cassman Brown* ([1973] EA 358. First, the court has to establish that there is an issue that requires determination. Secondly, the court must be satisfied that the applicant is likely to suffer damage if the injunction is not granted and finally, the court must consider if the balance of convenience favours grant of the injunction that is, court will have to weigh the potential injustice to the defendant if the injunction is granted. In *Paul Odalo Abuor v. Colour Print Ltd and Text Book Centre* (2002) Unreported, the court granted an ex parte order restraining Colour Print Ltd and Text Book Centre from printing, selling or distributing the plaintiff's book entitled *White Highlands No More: A Modern Political History of Kenya.* In *Jiwani Nevin v. Going Out Magazine & Another* Civil Suit No. 336 of 2003 the Court held in favour of the plaintiff and granted him an interim prohibitory injunction against the defendants whose works were infringing. In *Nevin Jiwani t/a Go Places Publications and Another, v. Yellow Pages Publishing and Marketing Ltd* [2006] eKLR, like the above cases, the courts took into account the principles laid down in *Anielo Giella v. Cassman Brown* to determine whether or not to grant injunctions.

(iii). Damages, Accounts for Profit, Delivery Up, Destruction and Reasonable Royalties

522. The rights holder may also seek damages for copyright infringement. Section 35(4) makes provisions for these remedies. These are meant to adequately compensate the rights holder for any losses occasioned by the infringement. Since IP is protected as any other proprietary rights in Kenya, the plaintiff is also entitled to other remedies that may be applicable in the case of other proprietary rights. The Court may also order the delivery up of the infringing items to the rights holder or destruction of the infringing works. In *Alternative Media Ltd v. Safaricom,* HCCC 263 of 2004, the court granted the plaintiff general damages of KES 100,000 and ordered the destruction of the remaining infringing scratch cards. In some instances, in lieu of damages, the court may award the plaintiff an amount based on the reasonable royalty which would have been payable by a licensee for the use of the works. This is mainly applicable in cases where the works are licensed to third parties. This can be a long process as the court may direct an enquiry to be held for purposes of determining the amount to be paid as reasonable royalty as this may not be easily available.

523. Article 46 of the TRIPS Agreement provides for the disposal of infringing works or equipment used to make infringing copies outside the channels of commerce. The court may order for the disposal of such goods in such a way that they should not find their way back into the market without compensating the person who committed the infringement. This is done in the presence of a court official or police to ensure that the goods are not diverted. When such destruction is done, a certificate of destruction will be issued. However, the laws provide a defence where these will not be applicable under section 35(5), which absolves the defendant from paying the damages, if he can prove that the time the infringement took place, the defendant was not aware of the infringement or had no reasonable grounds for suspecting that copyright subsisted in the work.

b. Criminal Sanctions

524. Article 51 provides that all members shall make provisions for criminal procedures and penalties to be applied in the case of wilful infringement done on a commercial scale. The laws should provide appropriate remedies, which include custodial sentences and fines that are deterrent. Section 38 of Cap. 130 makes it a criminal offence for one to sale or make for sale, distributes, imports infringing copies or has in his/her possession devices used for infringing copyright and related rights unless one acted in good faith. Unauthorised public performance of copyright-protected works will also amount to criminal infringement of copyright and one will be liable to fines, custodial sentences or both. The current fines were set in 2000 and are no longer deemed punitive or deterrent; a maximum of KES 800,000 for ten years or both. By 2015, the highest fine the courts gave for copyright infringement was KES 400,000 and the longest custodial sentence was six months.

525. Criminal actions are brought on behalf of the State by the KECOBO, which has copyright prosecutors specifically appointed to deal with copyright infringement cases. Once the case has been determined and the accused is found guilty, then the court will order the delivery up or destruction of the infringing goods. In *R v. Angeline Mbai* CF 2431 of 2000 (unreported) the magistrate held that the prosecution had failed to prove that the accused had committed an offence and acquitted him and ordered the exhibits be returned to her. The State did not appeal against this decision. Like all criminal cases, prosecution has to prove the case beyond reasonable doubt.

c. Evidence

526. Registration of copyright shall be prima facie evidence, of the particulars entered into the Copyright Register. The author is presumed to be the owner of the work unless the person purporting otherwise adduces evidence to the contrary.

5. Other Government Enforcement Agencies

527. Role of National Police Service in relation to copyright enforcement is similar to that of copyright inspectors within KECOBO. Under the law, they are empowered to enforce all the laws in Kenya. They have powers to search premises and seize infringing copies as well as arrest suspects in cases of suspected infringement of copyright. They work in collaboration with KECOBO and the Office of the Director of Public Prosecutions (DPP). Other Government Agencies that help with include the Department of Weights and Measures who enforce the Trade Descriptions Act, the Kenya Bureau of Standard and the ACA under the Anti-Counterfeit Act Cap. 130A of the Laws of Kenya.

528. The ACA is mandated to enforce IPR in Kenya. Under the Act, inspectors, including those from KECOBO are granted powers to seize counterfeit goods, and arrest alleged infringers. This shall be discussed in greater detail in the next section dealing with enforcement of trademarks.

6. Border Measures

529. Trade is goods and services across borders and in the global market has increased exponentially and covers electronic commerce as well. There is a need to have specific border measures to ensure that only legitimate products cross the borders. Articles 51 to 60 of the TRIPs Agreement and the World Customs Organisation Model Law require Members to provide adequate and effective border measures. Under section 26 of the Copyright Act, the author of a work or his successor in title has exclusive rights, to among other things, import their works. Border measures block entry of unauthorised copyright works before they are released into channels of commerce. These are effective when dealing with physical goods. Most copyright works are transmitted online to various digital platforms.

B. Trademarks

530. Enforcement of trade marks in Kenya is done through the KIPI, the ACA, Judiciary, Policy, Industry Organisations and other government agencies.

1. Kenya Industrial Property Office

531. The KIPI has a limited role in enforcement of trade marks as it mainly deals with the registration and administration of the same. The Registrar of Trade Marks has the authority to receive and determine opposition claims in relation to the application of a registered trade mark, which has been published in the gazette. Section 21 of the Trademarks Act Cap. 506 of the Laws of Kenya lays down the procedure in relation to opposition as to registration of a trade mark. It is important to note that where one is not satisfied with the Registrar's decision, he can file an appeal in court. Although the law creates offences, KIPI does not have the powers to deal with infringement and this as will be discussed below is one of the reasons that led to the creation of the ACA to deal with counterfeit goods.

2. Anti-Counterfeit Agency

532. The ACA was created under the Anti-Counterfeit Act, Cap. 130A of the Laws to deal with matters of counterfeit in Kenya. ACA has powers to investigate, prosecute and arrest persons alleged to be counterfeiting goods. This is done in collaboration with other enforcement agencies such as the National Police Service,

KECOBO, Kenya Bureau of Standards, Customs, Department of Weights and Measures among others. It is meant to coordinate the efforts of various agencies in enforcement of IPR although the main focus in counterfeit goods. Counterfeit goods are defined under section 2 of Cap. 130A as goods that are the result of counterfeiting, and includes any means used for purposes of counterfeiting;

a. Inspection, Seizure and Prosecution

533. In line with provisions of the TRIPs Agreement on enforcement, Cap. 130A makes provisions for appointment of inspectors from various agencies as designated by various acts of Parliament. These include the Standards Act Cap. 496, Weights and Measures Act Cap. 513, Copyright Act Cap. 130, Pharmacy and Poisons Act Cap. 244, Food, Drugs and Chemical Substances Act Cap. 254 and the Pest Control Act Cap. 346. This means that in addition to the inspectors specifically appointed under Cap. 130A, persons designated as inspectors including board members, police officers, customs personnel, trade development officers, trade mark and patent examiners, seed and plant inspector, Kenya Bureau of Standards Inspectors and copyright inspectors have the powers to inspect alleged counterfeit goods and premises in which they are stored.

534. Under section 23 of Cap. 130A, inspectors have the powers to inspect any premises of vehicle or place in which goods are suspected to be counterfeit or where counterfeiting is suspected to be taking place. They have the authority to terminate the manufacture or production of counterfeit goods but not destroy the same without following due process. They also have powers to seize and detain the suspect goods and store them as well as secure the same after taking an inventory. Interestingly, the Act grants inspectors powers to arrest without a warrant, which may be in contravention of current Constitution. The inspectors have full police powers and once goods have been seized, they have to be transported to the depot where they shall be securely stored awaiting court processes. Where a person is aggrieved by the actions of an inspector pursuant to the provisions of section 23, he may apply to a competent court for the goods for the relevant action. The Act makes it an offence for someone to impersonate an inspector and they will be liable to criminal action.

535. Once the complaint has been lodged, investigated, evidence has been secured and all procedures followed, ACA, through the DPP or prosecutors appointed by the DPP will proceed with the matter in court.

3. Compounding of Offences

536. The Executive Director, under section 34A of Cap. 130A has powers to order an alleged infringer, where an order for forfeiture is applicable, to pay a fine not exceeding the amount that the court would have fined had she or see been prosecuted in a court of law or order the forfeited goods to be destroyed. This provision, as desirable as it may be could be controversial as it grants the Executive Director powers similar to those granted by the court. This provision was included in the law in 2014 to provide, fast and expeditious remedies for the rights holder which is within the provisions of the TRIPs Agreement. The order is final leaving no room for the alleged infringer to appeal

C. *Judicial Proceedings*

537. Like in the case of copyright, the Judiciary plays an important role in enforcement of trademarks. As stated earlier, the right of appeal in the case of opposition proceedings lies in the High Court. The rights holders have the right to sue the alleged infringers or have criminal proceedings instituted through ACA and the DPP.

1. Civil Actions

538. Interestingly, Cap. 130A does not have specific provisions in relation to civil action and remedies and only makes reference in relation to evidence and presumption of ownership. The rights holders however have to rely on the Trade Marks act to institute civil actions against the alleged infringer. Section 46 of Cap. 506 provides that the certificate of registration shall be prima facie evidence of the validity of the original registration. Some infringement cases may involve the scope of registration and whether or not the alleged infringing mark is similar to the registered trademark or is likely to cause confusion. The rights holder is entitled to damages, injunctive relief and other orders such as forfeiture and destruction of infringing goods.

a. Injunctions

539. As discussed in the section on copyright above, the principles on which courts grant injunction in Kenya are laid down in *Anielo Giella v. Cassman Brown* ([1973] The rights holder may apply for injunctive relief to stop the alleged infringement. In *Pastificio Lucio Garofalo S.P.A v. Debenham & Fear Ltd* [2013] eKLR, the court granted injunctive relief in favour of the plaintiffs. The defendant was restrained from using the name *Santa Maria* for pasta, which was deemed to be similar to name *Santa Lucia,* a registered mark belonging to the plaintiff. Defendant's name was deemed to be similar to that of the plaintiff's mark and was likely to cause confusion among the users. In *Beiersdorf Ag v. Emirchem Products Limited* (Civil Case No. 559 of 2002) 1 KLR, the plaintiff, a limited liability company incorporated in Germany, – in which Beiersdorf East Africa Limited is the subsidiary – filed an interlocutory injunction against the defendant for infringement of its Trademark Number 32111 consisting of the word 'NIVEA'. The plaintiff claimed that the get-up of the jar in which the defendant marketed his product 'NIVELIN' – also a pure petroleum jelly – was so designed as to pass off the product as that of the plaintiff. Court held that the defendant's business was likely to cause irreparable damage to the plaintiff as such the plaintiff was granted an Interlocutory injunction against the defendant.

b. Damages, Delivery up and Destruction and Account for Profits

540. Cap. 506 does not have specific provisions on damages but this can be imputed from section 5. Damages are meant to restore the victim to the position they would have been had the infringement not taken place. One way of calculating the damages due is lost profits. The plaintiff may choose to have account for profits in lieu of damages. This deprives the defendant of any profits they have made as a result of the infringing action. The Court may order the infringer to delivery up of the goods or destruction. Delivery up is important as it ensures that the defendant does not divert the goods and they can be destroyed as appropriate as ordered by the court. This relief is applicable where the defendant still has the goods in his possession.

2. Criminal Cases

541. In many countries, infringement of trade marks is often dealt with under civil proceedings with few criminal infringement provisions and subsequent cases. Courts, or the Executive Director of the ACA as discussed in paragraph (b) above have the power to determine criminal infringement cases. Inspectors of the ACA institute criminal cases in relation to counterfeiting and they are prosecuted accordingly. The alleged infringer will be charged under section 24, 31 or 32. Any person who is convicted on an offence under section 32 of Cap. 130A is liable to fine not exceeding five times the value of the prevailing market price of the goods or a maximum jail term of fifteen years or both. The advantage of calculating the fine based on market value of the product times five is that it makes it punitive and deterrent and the law does not have to be changed to increase the fine. In the case of offences under section 24 or 31 of Cap. 130A, one will be liable to a term of imprisonment not exceeding three years or a fine not exceeding KES 2 million or both.

542. Offences created under sections 57 and 58 of Cap. 506 deal mainly with falsification of a trade mark and falsely representing a mark as registered. The fines and custodial sentences are relatively low and are unlikely to be punitive or deterrent. Section 58D and 58E deal with forgery of a trademark and importation of goods with a forged trade mark which will attract a fine of KES 2,000 or term of imprisonment not exceeding five years.

D. Customs and Border Measures

543. Border measures are crucial in enforcement of trade marks as the counterfeit goods can be prevented from entering the market right at the border. This requires co-operation from the Customs Department of the Kenya Revenue Authority. Section 34 of Cap. 130A clearly provides for border measures where the rights holder, who has valid reason to suspect that counterfeit goods are about to be imported into the country, may apply to the Commissioner of Customs to seize the goods for as long as the IP right subsists. The Commissioner shall deal with the application as appropriate once he or she is satisfied that the goods are prima facie protected goods, are protected by IP and the applicant is the owner. The duration of seizure and detention of goods shall be within the time set under the East African Community Customs Management Act of 2005. There are provisions to ensure that the applications are not malicious or false. The Commissioner is entitled to claim compensation from the applicant if the application proves to be false or malicious.

II. Patents/Industrial Designs/Utility Models

544. A patent, like all IPR is enforceable in court. The actions are mainly in relations to prevent the manufacture, sale and use of an invention protected under patents. It is important to note that enforcement of patent rights starts with the patenting process when the specifications of the patent are drafted and submitted to the patent office for examination. For one to determine a patent infringement, they may require expert witnesses and need to show that the alleged infringer has performed an action, which falls within the rights holder's control in relation to the patent. It includes independent, accidental or unintentional creation that is part of the protected works. Section 105 of the IPA Cap. 509 of the Laws of Kenya states that:

> Subject to sections 21(3) (e), 58, 61(6), 72, 73, 80(1) (c) and 86, any act specified under section 54 or 92 and performed by a person other than the owner of the patent of registered utility model or industrial design without the owner's authorisation in relation to a product of a process falling within the scope of a validly granted patent or certificate of registration shall constitute an infringement.

545. Infringement proceedings may be filed with the IPT or the High Court.

A. *Industrial Property Tribunal*

546. The IPT is a *quasi*-judicial body set up under section 113 of Cap. 509 with powers to listen to appeals arising from decisions of KIPI Managing Director in relation to registration of industrial property and infringement of patents, utility models and industrial designs. The owner of a patent, registered utility models and registered industrial design may request the IPT to grant relief in case of an infringement including injunctions in cases where an infringement that is about to occur or likely to occur or to stop an infringement that is already taking place. The Tribunal may also grant orders for damages to be paid by the infringer and any other remedy that is provided by law. The Tribunal, under section 106 of 509 becomes the 'court' of first instance when dealing with infringement as stated above.

547. On the other hand, a person, not a rights holder may seek orders from the Tribunal that his actions do not in any way constitute an infringement of the protected patent, registered utility model or registered industrial design and the rights holder will be listed as the defendant. Under section 107(2), the Tribunal will not grant the declaration if the acts are already subject to infringement proceedings or if the applicant is unable to prove that he had previously communicated with the rights holder and the rights holder had failed to respond in writing. This provision offers an opportunity for both parties to institute proceedings if they feel that they are aggrieved by the actions of the other party.

548. Where one is threatened with infringement proceedings and they can prove that their acts do not constitute and infringement of a patent, registered utility model or registered industrial design, may request and obtain an injunction to stop such threats from the Tribunal. The Tribunal may award damages for any losses incurred due to such threats. This provision underscores the complexity of patent infringement cases and the need to handle them well to avoid unnecessary losses. It offers a fast and expeditious remedy to infringement of patents, registered designs and registered utility models in Kenya.

549. The licensee of a patent registered utility model or registered industrial design may institute legal proceedings for infringement provided that they have notified the owner who has either consented or three months have lapsed since the request was made. The Tribunal under section 111(3) Cap. 509 may an injunction to stop the infringement where the licensee shows that the continuing infringement is likely to cause substantial damage. Any party to the proceedings at the Tribunal may appeal any order or decision made by the Tribunal in accordance with the rules set out under Cap. 509. The burden of proof in the proceedings, other than criminal proceedings falls on the infringer if the product is new and it is likely that the identical product was not made from the patented process and the patent holder has been unable, using reasonable means to determine the process used.

550. The Court's decision in *General Plastics Ltd v. The Industrial Property Tribunal and Another* acknowledged the role of the IPT as set out in the Act and they and the applicants should exercise their right under section 115 to appeal against the decision of the Tribunal.

B. Court Proceedings

551. The cost of patent litigation can be quite prohibitive and discourage rights holders from pursuing the cause of action. There are however cases that are filed in court including appeals from the decisions of the IPT. Issue of whether or not the court has jurisdiction to hear patent infringement cases was determined in *Naili East Africa Limited v. Samuel Kariuki & Patrick Odhiambo*[264] The plaintiff moved to court seeking an injunction to restrain the defendant from infringing on his protected patent: Aquatic Removal Method. The court held that it had no jurisdiction under sections 55, 105 and 106 of the IPA. The Court declined to grant the injunctive relief sought by the plaintiff and was of the opinion that the IPT should handle the matter as per the provisions of Cap. 509. It is notable that there are several cases that have been determined by the courts over the years. The decision asserted the

264. *Naili East Africa Ltd. v. Samuel Kariuki & Patrick Odhiambo* (HCCC 295 of 2014).

role of the Tribunal in determination of infringement cases as they relate to patents, registered utility models and registered industrial designs.

1. Civil Litigation

552. Does the court have jurisdiction to determine or hear infringement cases in the case of patents, registered utility models or registered designs? Until recently, the courts would hear and determine patent infringement cases as well either as the Court of First Instance or on Appeal. The court, may on determination of the case, grant an injunction to stop the infringement, and may award damages. In *Sanitam Services (EA) Ltd v. Rentokil (K) Ltd and Another,*[265] the applicant sought orders to restrain the respondents from offering for sale, selling and passing off the foot operated sanitary bins as theirs. The applicant was the legitimate owner of the patent. The Court declined to grant the injunction on grounds that applicant had failed to prove that there was an infringement and subsequently no proof that the applicant would suffer a loss. The applicant was not entitled to damages. If the case had been filed before the Tribunal, the outcome might have been different as under section 113(3) of Cap. 509 place the burden of proof on the infringer.

553. In *ENG Kenya Ltd v. Magnate Ventures Ltd*[266] [2009] eKLR, the plaintiff sought an injunction to restrain the defendant from using his registered industrial design pending the hearing and determination of the suit. The court granted an interlocutory injunction and ordered the defendant to remove all the suburban signs that he had erected within fourteen days. The court in making the decision took cognisance of the role of the Managing Director of KIPI and the IPT in determination of infringement cases as they relate to industrial designs.

2. Criminal Proceedings

554. Section 109 of Cap. 509 makes it an offence for a third party to intentionally infringe a patent, registered utility model or registered industrial design and will be liable to a fine not exceeding KES 50,000 or a jail term of not less than three years and not more than five years or both the fine and the jail term. The fines do not reflect the gravity of the criminal offence, as they were set more than thirty years ago and need to be revised.

C. Alternative Dispute Resolution

555. Alternative dispute resolution such as arbitration may be used for the determination of IP cases for several reasons. First, they take a shorter time to determine

265. *Sanitam Services (EA) Ltd. v. Rentokil (K) Ltd. and Another* Civil Case No.58 of 1999 [2000] KRL.
266. *ENG Kenya Ltd. v. Magnate Ventures Ltd.* [2009] eKLR.

and the parties are free to choose the arbitrator. Secondly, the costs tend to be relatively cheaper. Third, the decision of arbitrator is final so it reduces the time it will take to get to the final determination of the case. Parties may also opt for mediation, which is also cheaper and they can come to a mutual agreement.

D. Role of Industry Organisations

556. There are several industry organisations such as trade unions, associations and companies which also help in enforcement of IPR. They offer time, expertise and intelligence to the law enforcement agencies. Examples are the Kenya Association of Manufactures and the Recording Industry Association of Kenya.

E. Summary and Conclusion

557. For effective and expeditious enforcement of IP in Kenya, there is a need to have different approaches and use various institutions both in the public and private sector. It is important to have a clear strategy to deal with unauthorised commercial use of copyright-protected works, counterfeiting and infringement of patents, registered utility models and registered industrial designs. Administrative measures, civil remedies and criminal sanctions all play an important role. The TRIPS Agreement clearly states that Members need not set up specialised courts to deal with IP infringement cases. It is crucial to have enforcement agencies with well-informed and specialised inspectors, prosecutors, Judges, magistrates, lawyers as well as rights holders.

558. Penalties for offences created under the various acts should be punitive and deterrent as is the case of the Anti-Counterfeit Act Cap. 130A of the laws of Kenya which does not set a specific amount but provides that the fines should be based on the prevailing market price of the goods, multiplied by a certain factor and the total number of infringed works. The cost of litigation may be prohibitive and it is important for the rights holders to weigh the options and where possible institute criminal proceedings that might deter the infringer even if the rights holder does not get compensated for the damage suffered.

Selected Bibliography

Books

Abbot F et al., *The International Intellectual Property System: Commentary and Materials,* Hague, Kluwer International (1999).

Bently L. Sherman B, *Intellectual Property* Law, 4th Edition, UK, Oxford University Press, (2014).

Tune C, *Copyright Licensing Fundamentals,* Understanding the Intellectual Property License #14730 (2008).

Fisher W, *Theories of International Property* (2001).

Mwakikagile G, *Kenya: Identity of a Nation*, Pretoria, SA: New African Press (2007).

Julie C et al., *Copyright in a Global Economy*, New York, Aspen Law (2002).

Nonini, D.M., *The Global Idea of the 'Commons',* Berghahn Books, New York (2007).

O'Connor B, *The Law of Geographical Indications* London, CMP Publishing Ltd (2004).

Paul G, *Copyright's Highway*, Stanford, Stanford University Press (2003).

Book Chapters

Blackeney M, 'Geographical Indications' in Blackeney M. et al. (eds), *Extending the Protection of Geographical Indications: Case Studies of Agricultural Products in Africa,* London Earthscan from Routledge (2012).

Journal Articles

Ginsburg. J, *A Tale of Two Copyrights: Literary Property in Revolutionary France and America*, 64 *Tul. L. Rev.* 991, 992 (1990).

Nzomo, V. & Rutenberg, I, *'Patenting the Un-Patentable? A review of patentable subject matter in granted patent claims: Kenya as a case study,'* 5 South African Intellectual Property Law Journal, 58–74 (2017).

Reports

Food and Agriculture Organization of the United States, *International Treaty on Plant Genetic Resources for Food and Agriculture.*

http://www.fao.org/fileadmin/user_upload/legal/docs/033s-e.pdf.

Selected Bibliography

Government of Kenya, *Kenya 2009 Population and Housing Census Analytical Report on Population Dynamics*, Vol. III, Kenya Population Situation Analysis, (2013).

UK IPRs Commission Report, *Integrating IPRs and Development Policy*, (2002).

World Intellectual Property Organization, *Case Study: Hoodia Plant*: http://www.wipo.int/export/sites/www/academy/en/about/global_network/educational_materials/cs1_hoodia.pdf

Publications

WIPO, *Geographical Indications an Introduction.*

WIPO, *Intellectual Property Handbook: Policy, Law and Practice.*

WIPO, *Intellectual Property Handbook: Policy Law and Use.*

Theses

Ouma M., *Enforcement of Copyright and Related Rights in the Music industry on sub Saharan Africa*, PhD Thesis, Queen Mary University of London (2010).

Conference Papers

WIPO Briefing Paper No. 2, *The WIPO Intergovernmental Committee on Intellectual Property and Genetic Resources, Traditional Knowledge and Folklore*: https://www.wipo.int/export/sites/www/tk/en/resources/pdf/tk_brief2.pdf.

Online Resources

Kenya Copyright Board: www.copyright.go.ke/.

Kenya Industrial Property Institute: www.kipi.go.ke/.

World Intellectual Property Organization: www.wipo.int/portal/en/index.html.

Kenya Plant Health Inspectorate: www.kephis.org.

Anti-Counterfeit Authority: www.aca.go.ke.

Central Intelligence Agency (CIA), The World Factbook, Kenya Chapter, 2009 Estimates: www.cia.gov/library/publications/the-world-factbook/geos/ke.html.

Maps

Survey of Kenya, Ministry of Lands, Government of Kenya.

Index

The numbers given refer to paragraph numbers.

Index

Index

Made in the USA
Monee, IL
18 October 2026

66041417R10098